CAE Result

Teacher's Pack

Karen Ludlow

A70778

OXFORD

UNIVERSITY PRESS

OXFORD

UNIVERSITY PRESS

Great Clarendon Street, Oxford OX2 6DP

Oxford University Press is a department of the University of Oxford.
It furthers the University's objective of excellence in research, scholarship,
and education by publishing worldwide in

Oxford New York

Auckland Cape Town Dar es Salaam Hong Kong Karachi
Kuala Lumpur Madrid Melbourne Mexico City Nairobi
New Delhi Shanghai Taipei Toronto

With offices in

Argentina Austria Brazil Chile Czech Republic France Greece
Guatemala Hungary Italy Japan Poland Portugal Singapore
South Korea Switzerland Thailand Turkey Ukraine Vietnam

OXFORD and OXFORD ENGLISH are registered trade marks of
Oxford University Press in the UK and in certain other countries

ISBN: 978 0 19 480040 2

Printed in China

ACKNOWLEDGEMENTS

Pages 132–134 reproduced with the kind permission of Cambridge ESOL.

Contents

Introduction

Course overview

CAE Result is a shorter, contemporary and attractively designed course with unusual, eye-catching artwork. It covers the major language skills, and provides students with comprehensive preparation for the Cambridge Certificate in Advanced English (revised December 2008) at the Council of Europe C1 level. Its lively, up-to-date texts are all from authentic sources, such as newspapers, magazines, brochures and books, and include interviews and radio programmes. Its engaging topics are designed to stimulate interest and provoke discussion.

Each unit of the course has a general topic heading, but each section within the unit is free-standing and has a different angle on the overall topic. This gives teachers flexibility in planning lessons and provides variety for students. There is an emphasis on grammar and vocabulary work throughout the course and a review section at the end of each unit which allows students to check what they have learned. Dictionary skills work is integrated throughout the Student's Book and Workbook, with additional support in the *Using a dictionary for exams* booklet in the Teacher's Pack (see page 7 of this Introduction).

As well as being encouraged to consolidate, improve and activate their knowledge of the English language, students are given extensive training in all CAE examination skills and task types. The *How to do it* boxes offer general help in tackling these task types, and in building on their language skills, while the *Tip* boxes give additional helpful hints on how to approach individual tasks.

The flexibility, organisation and additional components of the course enable it to be used with students studying several hours a week throughout the academic year, or with students on shorter, more intensive courses.

The course consists of a Student's Book, class audio cd, a Teacher's Pack, and Workbook Resource Packs (with or without key).

Course components

The Student's Book

The course consists of 12 units, each of which is divided into these sections:

- Lead in
- Reading
- Vocabulary
- Grammar
- Use of English
- Writing
- Review

The Lead in sections are designed to introduce, through a variety of skills input and activities, the various sub-topics and key vocabulary of the unit. The eye-catching pages with their stimulating activities will motivate students so that they approach each unit with enthusiasm.

The Reading sections deal comprehensively with all the Reading task types. There is a short lead in question before students tackle the exam task and sometimes a short exercise based on the vocabulary in the text itself, although students are not encouraged to find out the precise meaning of all the words in the text. The last exercise often invites students to react to what they have just read.

The Vocabulary sections draw on and expand topic or lexico-grammatical vocabulary from the Lead in, Reading or Use of English pages, and encourage students to use the vocabulary in context. As well as topic-related vocabulary, there are functional phrases, useful expressions, easily confused words, word formation and phrasal verbs. Many of these sections encourage students to refer to a dictionary, and a number of exercises are designed to show students how a dictionary can help specifically with exam tasks, as well as generally supporting their language learning, and helping them to become more independent learners.

The Grammar sections adopt a holistic approach to grammar, tackling general areas by checking what students already know, and then inviting them to practise newly acquired knowledge. The sections are cross-referenced to the Grammar Reference at the back of the Student's Book.

The Listening sections introduce the topic in question and encourage students to react to what they have heard. The tasks cover all the CAE Listening task types and students are encouraged to build on their listening skills in a variety of ways, e.g. by deciding why answers are wrong.

The Speaking sections focus on a particular part of the Speaking test. Students are invited to listen to recordings of other students doing the different parts of the Speaking test, evaluate the students' performances, then tackle the tasks themselves. As well as in the *How to do it* boxes, help is also given in the form of groups of phrases, e.g. *Answering personal questions*, which students can use when doing the tasks. Colourful artwork also appears in the form of illustrations or pictures used for the exam tasks. Wherever possible, the pictures have been given a prominent position on the page to facilitate their use for exam tasks.

As well as highlighting the individual task types, care has been taken to make the Use of English sections as interesting and stimulating as possible. Each section covers one or more of the five task types and most also focus on another aspect of language, e.g. spelling and punctuation, grammar or vocabulary. Dictionary skills work, similar to that in the vocabulary sections, also features here.

The Writing sections deal comprehensively with the compulsory Part 1 question and all the choices in the Part 2 examination task types. Models of good and less effective writing styles are given and students are invited to analyse these, practise their writing skills at sentence or paragraph level, then produce a complete piece of writing of their own.

The Review sections test the main vocabulary work studied in the unit. Several short exercises invite students to revise the highlighted vocabulary sections and main writing focus, and identify any areas requiring further study. They provide a valuable progress check at regular intervals and can be done in class or set for homework, depending on the time available.

The Exam Overview outlines comprehensively what each part of the CAE exam consists of, how long each paper lasts and the number of marks awarded, and explains the grading system or criteria for assessment, where applicable. Each paper is broken down into the following:

- the number of items, sections or task types in each part
- what you do in each part
- what each part tests

Cross-references to the *How to do it* boxes on the relevant pages of the Student's Book are given here.

The Writing Guide gives students additional support with further questions, model answers and guidance for writing letters, contributions, magazine articles, competition entries, reviews, essays, reports and proposals, as well as the set text option.

The Grammar Reference provides comprehensive rules and explanations for the usage of individual grammar items, namely: tenses, future forms, non-continuous verbs, passives, gerunds and infinitives, relative clauses, direct and indirect speech, modals, participle clauses, conditionals, wishes and regrets, comparatives and superlatives, emphasis, and the grammar of phrasal verbs.

The Appendix contains additional material for certain pages of the Student's Book, e.g. extra information, answers and pictures for Speaking activities.

The Teacher's Pack

The Teacher's Pack consists of a Teacher's Book with DVD, a *Writing and Speaking Assessment Booklet* and a *Using a dictionary for exams* booklet.

The Teacher's Book contains procedural notes and a full answer key, including suggested answers, for the activities in the Student's Book. It also includes the tapescripts for the listening sections with highlighted answers, as well as optional activities for classroom use. There are 12 Unit Tests and four Progress Tests with answer keys, which can be photocopied for classroom use. At the back of the Teacher's Book there is information about www.oxfordenglishtesting.com .

The 32-page *Writing and Speaking Assessment Booklet* is divided into two sections. The Writing section contains information about the assessment criteria used by Cambridge ESOL for marking Paper 2 answers, and has an authentic sample answer, written by a student studying at CAE level, for each of the tasks in the Writing sections of the Student's Book. Each answer is accompanied by notes on the requirements of the task, and an assessment of the answer according to the examiner's criteria.

The Speaking section specifically supports the DVD, which contains footage of real students doing Paper 5 tests under exam conditions, with commentaries and analysis by experienced oral examiners. The DVD is designed to help teachers in a number of ways: to familiarise them with the format of the Speaking Paper; to explain the requirements of each Part and the assessment criteria used by the examiners; to enable them to assess their own students and be able to train them to give a good performance. Sections of the DVD can also be shown in class to students, using the photocopiable worksheets in the booklet at the same time.

The 32-page *Using a dictionary for exams* booklet complements the dictionary work that features throughout the Student's Book and Workbook. Aimed at teachers of PET, FCE and CAE, it contains ideas for classroom activities for each of the main papers in these exams, showing how dictionaries can help with specific exam tasks. The 11 worksheets are photocopiable for use in class.

The Workbook Resource Pack

The Workbook Resource Pack consists of a Workbook (with or without key) and a MultiROM. The MultiROM at the back of the Workbook contains audio material linked to the Listening Sections in the Workbook. Students can play the audio in a CD player or on a computer. There is also a link which launches students to www.oxfordenglishtesting.com where they get access to two interactive online CAE practice tests. The tests offer authentic CAE practice, automatic marking for instant results and an online dictionary look-up facility. For further information, please see the section about the website at the back of this Teacher's Book or visit the website itself.

The Workbook consists of the same number of units as the Student's Book and mirrors the examination task types. The umbrella topics are the same as those in the Student's Book but the section topics are different, although they have some connection to those in the Student's Book. Each unit consists of five sections: Reading, Vocabulary, Grammar, Listening and Use of English.

Vocabulary and Grammar are given a high profile. The Vocabulary sections pick up on and extend the vocabulary introduced in the Reading texts.

Grammar both consolidates what has been taught in the Student's Book, e.g. a review of verb patterns, and

introduces further mini-grammar sections, e.g. adjective and adverb order, in the Grammar Extra sections.

The Listening and Use of English sections give students further practice in exam task types.

Dictionary skills work also features in the Vocabulary and Use of English sections.

Workbook Review sections

After every three units, i.e 1–3, 4–6, 7–9, 10–12, there is a two-page review of the vocabulary and grammar in the three previous units. These enable students to check their own progress at regular intervals and identify any areas requiring further study.

Writing

The Writing section starting on page 84 consists of an additional task for each of the 12 units. The tasks mirror those in the Student's Book.

Speaking

The MultiROM accompanying the Workbook also contains authentic recordings of students doing Paper 5 tasks from the Student's Book with the relevant photos reproduced in the Workbook. Students can analyse and evaluate the performances they hear. There are different kinds of activities for students to complete while they are listening to the recordings. This will help them consolidate what they have learned about the requirements of the Speaking Test and help them to improve their own performances.

There is also a complete Speaking test for students to listen to and evaluate at www.oup.com/elt/result. The speaking practice is also complemented by the DVD with the *Writing and Speaking Assessment Booklet* in the Teacher's Pack (see page 7 of this Introduction).

Website materials

Additional materials are available on the Result Teacher's site www.oup.com/elt/teacher/result and on the Student's site at www.oup.com/elt/result.

What are you like?

Lead in p9

1 In pairs or small groups ask students to compare their ideal jobs and any qualities they think might be necessary for the jobs they choose, e.g. *designer: you'd have to be pretty creative and innovative.* Make a class list of nouns/adjectives for job qualities and check pronunciation and word stress.

2 Before students do the quiz, check they understand the phrasal verbs in the text (*break out, get on with, stick with*) and other words or expressions as appropriate (*mingle, leap in, get stuck*). Refer students to the key on page 153 and make sure they understand the scoring system.

Suggested answer

Students may suggest the quiz isn't accurate because it tends to offer two extreme options and a more measured response for each situation or problem. They may also feel that the jobs suggested require other skills or abilities rather than personality traits, or that there is too much overlap or contradiction in the results.

Reading p10

1 Explain that for Reading Part 3 it is useful to read through the whole text quite quickly first, in order to get a general overview before looking at the multiple-choice questions (see the first point in the *How to Do It* box). Give students a time limit of approximately three minutes to help them with speed reading and to encourage them not to get stuck on vocabulary they may not know or may not need to know.

Suggested answers

1 Psychometric tests have increased in popularity in many areas.

2 The author thinks the tests may not always be accurate, but says they are very compulsive and appeal to our belief that we can find a perfect answer to everything.

3 Tests like the Myers-Briggs Type Indicator are used by many large companies to select staff for appropriate jobs but may not be scientifically accurate.

4 Some psychologists criticise these type of tests because employers tend to look for the same kind of personality type. Cheating in these tests is pointless because you will have to fake a personality you don't have.

5 Personality tests may have some advantages because they show us the reality of what we are, not what we may want to be.

2 Point out that this task is useful for focusing on detail in order to distinguish between similar reasons, outcomes or opinions, and to prevent misunderstandings. Refer students to the *How to do it* box at the top of the page and suggest they follow the advice as they do the task.

Key

2 A ✓ *I am mainly motivated by peace. I might have been more convinced about this …* (l.-45–49). This implies the writer isn't necessarily always a 'peaceful' person.

B ✗ The author doesn't imply the types of activity in the test are especially challenging. (l. 35–44).

C ✗ The author says the tests are incredibly compulsive, you can get hooked on them (l.-34) and she was willing to spend 40 minutes doing one. (l. 37).

D ✗ The author believes the tests are compulsive and you can get hooked on them but she doesn't imply they are too personal. (l. 33–34).

3 A ✗ *we are born with a predisposition to one personality type.* (l. 57–58).

B ✗ There is no reference to this.

C ✓ (l. 57–58).

D ✗ There is no reference to this.

4 A ✗ There is no reference to this.
   B ✗ David Bartram says there is no point in lying. (l. 80–84).
   C ✓ (l. 72–78).
   D ✗ Organisations want people with the same traits. (l. 69–72).

5 A ✗ There is no reference to this.
   B ✓ (l. 94–98).
   C ✗ This opinion is expressed by Dr Gill (l.-68–73).
   D ✗ (see l. 96–98)

3 Encourage students to look at the words in context to help them choose the correct meaning. Remind them that it is useful to check for and note down any collocations or dependent prepositions when verifying meaning, e.g. *an indicator of performance*, *strong emotions*, *a blazing row*.

Key

a 3 b 4 c 1 d 6 e 2 f 5

4 With younger students, ask if any of them spend time doing personality tests online or in magazines, and what they think of them. Older students might have had experience of these tests when applying for a job.

Background information

The Myers-Briggs Type Indicator (MBTI) is a psychological test which aims to help a person identify their personality by selecting preferences. Katherine Briggs and her daughter Isabel Myers developed the test during World War II, based on the theories of the psychoanalyst Carl Jung.

Vocabulary p12

1 Ask students if any of the adjectives they chose for Exercise 1 page 9 are the same as those here.

Key

a 3 b 9 c 5 d 10 e 1 f 4 g 8 h 7 i 6 j 2

2 Students may not necessarily agree about which adjectives are positive or negative. Encourage them to give reasons why with examples.

Suggested answers

+	+ /–	–
mature	sensitive	introvert
decisive	ambitious	
motivated	inquisitive	
conscientious		
extrovert		
independent		

3 It's important to encourage students to refer to dictionaries wherever possible in and out of class. An awareness of meaning in context, parts of speech, prefixes, suffixes, synonyms and antonyms help students when dealing with specific exam tasks.

For an introduction to using dictionaries, see pages 2 and 3 in the *Using a dictionary for exams* booklet in the Teacher's Pack.

Key

a frank/blunt/direct b outspoken c open/frank

4 You might want to set a time limit for discussion of up to four minutes to get students accustomed to timing for Speaking Part 4.

Grammar p12

1 Key
   a present perfect continuous, present perfect simple
   b present continuous, present simple
   c past simple, past perfect simple
   d future continuous, future simple
   e past simple, past perfect continuous
   f present simple, present continuous
   g past continuous, past simple

Optional Activity

Students should be able to complete exercise 1 easily, but if necessary write some sentences about yourself on the board using as many of the tenses from exercise 1 as possible, and ask students to identify which tense is used and why, e.g.

a I live in (place).
b I've been living here for (how long).
c I (had finished my university degree) before I (started-work).
d I (was working in a library) when I (applied for this job).
e Since I (started work here), I've (made a lot of new friends).

2 For c), d), e) and g), tell students to think carefully about the order of actions/events. Encourage them to explain the order in their own words, e.g. c 1: *As I left the house it started raining. When I left the house it was already raining.*

Key

a In the first sentence, the speaker is still learning to drive but in the second sentence, the speaker has finished learning and can now drive.

b In the first sentence, Carla is playing the guitar at the time of speaking. In the second sentence, the action is a general truth.

c In the first sentence, it started raining at the same time as I left the house. In the second sentence, it was already raining when I left.

d In the first sentence, the speaker will already be preparing the meal when the other person arrives. In the second sentence, the speaker will prepare the meal after the person arrives.

e In the first sentence, the person cried at the moment when the others arrived at the house. In the second sentence, the person had been crying before the others arrived.

f In the first sentence the speaker is explaining a fact. In the second sentence the speaker is emphasising that the action is continuous and is probably expressing annoyance.

g In the first sentence, the party was already happening when she made the announcement. In the second sentence, they had a party as a result of the announcement.

3 Key

a had been digging
b Is your father working ... ?
c had
d will take
e was leaving
f have been having
g will be travelling
h has broken down
i spend

4 Remind students that certain verbs are never used in the continuous form and that some of the most common of these are verbs which express a)-thoughts or opinions, b) likes or preferences, or c) states or possession.

Refer students to the section on non-continuous verbs in the Grammar Reference page 169 before they do tasks 4–6.

Key

a	Do they belong ... ?	e	hated
b	smell	f	contains
c	deserve	g	✓
d	✓	h	belong

5 Point out that verbs of perception (*hear, taste, see,* etc.) are often used with *can.* Once students have completed the task, ask them to produce sentences to illustrate differences in meaning for the verbs they think can take both forms, e.g. *What does 'laid-back' mean in English? We've been meaning to buy a good dictionary but we haven't had time yet.*

Key

a like   hear
believe   understand
know   belong
remind   contain
detest   prefer

b taste
'This food tastes delicious!' (have a good flavour)
'I'm just tasting the soup to see if it has enough salt.' (try)
mean
'We don't know what it means.' (represent/ signify)
'I've been meaning to phone you but I haven't had time.' (intend)

6 Key

a	5 (taking part in)		f	7 (considering)
b	8 (seems to be)		g	9 (interests)
c	3 (holding/attending)		h	4 (asking for)
d	2 (possesses)		i	1 (meeting)
e	6 (believes)		j	10 (observe)

7 Key

a feel
b was smelling
c don't see
d have had
e Do you think ... ?

8 Remind students that error analysis can be useful for improving their own written work and that it is advisable for them to check their own and classmates' written work regularly for all types of errors.

Key

Hi, my name's Michele. I was born in Geneva, but I have been living/have lived in Rome for the past ten years or so. I moved here because I wanted to be nearer my grandparents. I trained as a nurse after I('d) left school but I haven't actually found a job in nursing yet. At the moment I'm doing temporary work in an office but I'm thinking of taking a year out next year to travel and see the world. I enjoy outdoor sports and dancing, and I love all sorts of music but especially jazz and reggae. I played in a band when I was a student and I still perform in public when I get the chance. As regards my personality, I think I'm quite easy to get on with. I'm laid-back, and I have a great sense of humour.

Optional activity

Ask students if they ever write letters or if they use email and mobile phone texting more often. Ask who they usually write to, and ask them to consider some of the differences in layout and style for writing letters, emails and texting. Ask what kind of mistakes they might make when writing emails. Refer students to the Writing Guide on page 155 for examples of the different layouts for different types of written text.

Suggested answers

Emails are informal in style.

Texting reduces language to codes so students don't have to worry about spelling/punctuation/style, etc.

The kind of mistakes students particularly tend to make when writing emails are with spelling and punctuation, as well as grammatical errors.

9 After writing, suggest students check each other's emails for possible errors.

Listening p14

1 Check that students recognise and can name the activities shown in the photos (1 mosaic making 2 paintballing 3 car restoration 4 photography 5 singing). Ask if any of them do/have done these activities. Encourage them to use any vocabulary from the Lead in and Reading sections, e.g. *You might take up photography because you're a creative person.*

2 Explain to students that in Listening Part 4 they will listen to five speakers talking about a common theme. They will probably have to recognise the purpose of what is said as well as the speakers' attitudes and opinions. Allow students a little time to read through phrases a–g before listening.

Key

1 b   2 d   3 e   4 a   5 c   6 g   7 f

Tapescript

1	I got so carried away with it all.
2	I'd been made redundant.
3	I was babbling on about my workload.
4	There was a real mixed bag of us.
5	You could have knocked me down with a feather.
6	I was at a bit of a loose end.
7	I'd been having a bit of a rough time workwise.

3 Remind students that they have a short amount of time (up to about a minute) before the recording starts. They should use this time to read through the tasks carefully.

Key

1 E   2 H   3 F   4 D   5 B   6 D   7 H   8 B
9 G   10 C

Tapescript

Speaker 1
I ended up doing a photography course at the local college. Earlier in the year, I'd been made redundant and **I was at a bit of a loose end** – so it was my birthday present to myself! I was a bit apprehensive about going along alone – but I'm an outgoing type, and there was a real mixed bag of us, from beginners to those who'd been doing it for years. For me it was like a second childhood. In the first six weeks, I'd taken about a hundred photographs – I've even exhibited some. Now it's not just a hobby – **it's a totally compulsive activity** for me!

Speaker 2

I'd been having a bit of a rough time workwise. I'd been sketching for years, so a friend suggested I should go on a fine arts course, which included mosaic making. Eventually, I booked myself onto one, but I was terrified I wouldn't be as good as everyone else. As it turned out, I needn't have worried because everyone worked at their own pace. Anyway, I produced this weird abstract mosaic. It started out as a kind of nightmare scenario – very gloomy. Then I slowly added more colour, realising that **the depressing thoughts that had originally bothered me enough to inspire the design no longer mattered to me so much.** It finished up being rather like therapy.

Speaker 3

I was getting over an operation and felt the need to be out and about. As luck would have it, I saw a paintballing centre advertised in the local newspaper. 'Just what I need,' I thought. '**A nice bit of physical activity** and fun at the weekends!' Not that I was keen on sports – but I thought 'Why not?' Well, I got so carried away with it all that I decided to try and get into the local team. Well, you've guessed it, I didn't exactly become a mega-star overnight. But there's always next season! In the meantime, I'm starting to enjoy other kinds of sports, and **I've become much more determined to win** too.

Speaker 4

Now there's no way I'm mechanically minded but **I decided I needed a little diversification in life.** I certainly didn't need an activity to take me away from a desk job – I'm a climbing instructor! But I happened to see an old Volkswagen Beetle advertised in the window of our local newsagent's and decided to take a look at it. It was a bit of a wreck but I bought it anyway. Well, you should have seen it when I'd finished working on it. Restored to its former glory it's a real collector's piece. I think **what I discovered from the experience was a completely different side of myself** – a side I never even knew I had!

Speaker 5

I've always been into music. I play the guitar and sing – I even worked as a DJ in Spain, once! Well one day, I was babbling on about my workload, when my brother suggested I recorded a CD. I thought he was mad but **I didn't want to upset him** by saying so. Well, that was it! My first CD took me 18 months to record. I even wrote the songs myself. I suppose a professional singer would pick up on the flaws! Anyway, I sent it to a couple of record companies – never really thinking anyone would listen to it, or that **it would eventually make me as much money as it did.** You could have knocked me down with a feather when one of them contacted me to say they were interested! It's certainly inspired me to do some more recordings!

4 Remind students that this type of question is common in Speaking Part 1. Encourage them to expand on ideas and give reasons why/how often/with whom/where they enjoy doing the interests they talk about.

Speaking p15

1 Refer students back to the email on page 13 to check if any of the personal information links to the questions (a–f). Encourage them to try to use at least two of the useful phrases in *Answering personal questions* while they do the task.

2 Encourage students to correct the tense and explain why it is incorrect.

Key

1 I'm doing: present continuous for present actions, not present simple.
2 I've been (living) here: present perfect continuous for unfinished past, not present simple.
3 I enjoy: present simple for facts, not present continuous.
4 I have: present simple for personal attributes, not present continuous.
5 I visited: past simple for finished past actions, not present perfect simple.

Tapescript

Conversation 1
Q: What do you do?
A: At the moment I do a part-time job.
Conversation 2
Q: How long have you been living here?
A: I'm here for six years.
Conversation 3
Q: What do you enjoy doing in your spare time?
A: I'm enjoying going to the cinema.
Conversation 4
Q: How would you describe yourself?
A: I think I'm having an outgoing character.
Conversation 5
Q: What did you do last summer?
A: I've visited the mountains.

3 Check students understand the useful phrases in *Asking for personal information* and encourage them to use these when asking questions a–e. Encourage them to think of one or two more question types to practise further, e.g. hopes and plans for the future, reasons for studying English.

4 Remind students that it is important not to give one-word answers, but to expand on information. Where possible they should try to give reasons or examples from personal experience.

Suggested answers

Although there is nothing intrinsically wrong with this exchange, this is a very half-hearted, uninspiring effort. The first candidate initially says she doesn't know. She then mentions two activities but doesn't expand on her ideas much. She does encourage her partner by asking him about his leisure activities. Candidate 2's 'Nothing much' answer shows a lack of enthusiasm and doesn't really demonstrate language abilities. Candidates can improve their performance by including more information about when/why/how often or not/ who he/she does activities with. If candidates don't have time for leisure activities, they should try and explain why.

Tapescript

Examiner:	What are your interests and leisure activities?
Candidate 1:	I don't know really – maybe tennis and watching TV.
Candidate 1:	Oh, nothing much. I like the cinema.

5 While students are practising in pairs, monitor to make sure both are giving sufficient answers and one isn't dominating the conversation. You might want to give students a time limit of one to two minutes per question.

6 Ask students whether they can add to the candidates' arguments for learning another language.

Suggested answers

This is a good response. The candidate has quickly thought of something to say and can express her ideas confidently using a range of vocabulary.

Tapescript

Examiner:	How important do you think it is to learn another language?
Candidate:	Oh, from my point of view, it's absolutely essential. We live in an international community nowadays and we can communicate with people on the other side of the world in a matter of minutes. But, in my opinion, learning another language isn't just useful or even fascinating – I personally feel that it's also a mark of respect for the people you're communicating with.

There is authentic practice of this section on page 92 of the Workbook.

Use of English p16

1 Students discuss their ideas in pairs. Encourage them to think of any personal anecdotes or stories.

2 Ask students to read through the text quickly to get a general overview. Check the meaning of *showered them with praise*. Ask students if anything surprised them. Refer them to the *How to do it* box before starting the task.

Key

1	adjective	6	noun
2	noun	7	adjective
3	adjective	8	adjective
4	noun	9	noun
5	noun	10	adverb

3 Remind students that spelling is important when completing this task. Students might want to check possible answers in a dictionary.

Key

1	psychological	6	expectations
2	personality	7	gifted
3	approachable	8	exceptional
4	variety	9	encouragement
5	possibilities	10	undeniably

For extra practice with dictionaries and Use of English, Part 3, see Worksheet 8 in the *Using a dictionary for exams* booklet in the Teacher's Pack.

4 Encourage students to look carefully at the dictionary entry in order to make their decisions.

Key

1 b
2 a
3 c

Optional Activity

Write the sentences below on the board and ask students to complete the gaps with *make* or *bring*. Encourage them to check in a dictionary and discuss the different meanings of the verbs in context.

1 We asked the waiter to _____ us the bill.
2 Did you _____ that cake? You're a good cook!
3 They _____ quality goods at this company.
4 Climate change is expected to _____ chaos.
5 I don't think we're going to _____ it on time.

Key

bring
1 go and get something
4 cause
make
2 cook
3 produce
5 arrive

---

5 Refer students to the *How to do it* box before doing the task. Once they have decided on the missing words, encourage them to look at them in context and explain their meaning.

Key

a doubt
b prove

Vocabulary p17

1 Encourage students to check dictionaries for this type of exercise.

Key

a 6 no such luck
b 1 push your luck
c 5 the luck of the draw
d 4 take pot luck
e 8 are out of luck
f 7 with any luck
g 2 by a stroke of luck
h 3 beginner's luck

Optional Activity

Before students discuss the questions in exercise 2, tell them a good or bad luck story based on personal experience. Encourage them to ask questions about the chain of events and, if possible, guess the final outcome.

Writing p18

1 Explain to students that the Writing Part 2 task is compulsory. Refer them to the Exam Overview on page 5 and the Writing Guide on page 155 for more information on the possible task types in the exam.

Key

a To an international holiday company. To give a character reference for a friend.
b How long you have known the person; a detailed description of the person's character; the reasons why he/she would be suitable for the job.

2 Explain that this is a useful brainstorming activity which will help them to later structure their argument and organise their ideas.

Suggested answers

a Organise arrivals and departures at airports, give information, entertain, deal with problems, deal with complaints/difficult customers, organise trips/excursions, act as a guide on sightseeing trips, translate, etc.

b The ability to speak good English or other languages, organisational skills, listening skills, knowledge of local area and local customs, etc.

c Tact, patience, energy, a sense of humour, conscientiousness, etc.

3 Remind students that making a plan before writing is important for the organisation of points and paragraphs, and, although it may seem time-consuming, can actually help to save time by preventing them running out of ideas halfway through writing.

Suggested answer

The writer of A did not make a plan. She jumps from point to point and sometimes repeats herself (*sport* is referred to in paragraph 4 and again in paragraph 6; David's ability to deal with difficult people is referred to in paragraph 5 and again in paragraph 8.) There is little variety in sentence structure either (*Juan is, Juan doesn't, Juan speaks, Juan works*, etc.) This affects the flow of the text for the reader.

4 Point out that apart from a lack of organisation, letter A also uses words and expressions that are too informal (*certainly knows how to enjoy life, a complete extrovert, a laid-back person, stay cool*, etc.)

Suggested answers

a The writer of B makes better use of linking words: *who, and, so, because, although, for this reason, if, as well as, in addition to.*
Linking words in A: *and, but.*

b Paragraph 1: describes the organisational skills and personal qualities of the person recommended.
Paragraph 2: describes the skills and qualities of the person in relation to entertainment.
Paragraph 3: describes the skills and qualities of the person in relation to sports activities.
Paragraph 4: sums up the recommendation.

c Dear Sir or Madam
To whom it may concern
I am writing to you on behalf of …
I have known … for … years.
I have no hesitation in recommending him/her (for the post).
Yours faithfully

5 Encourage students to follow the advice in the boxes. Remind them to use any notes they made on adjectives and nouns for describing personality and/or skills from the Lead in and Reading sections. Refer students to the Writing Guide on page 155 for further help with the format and conventions for formal letters.

For an assessed authentic answer to this Writing task, see page 6 of the *Writing and Speaking Assessment Booklet* in the Teacher's Pack.

Review p20

1 Key
a 3 b 8 c 4 d 1 e 6 f 7 g 2 h 5

2 Key

a	tactful	e	cautious
b	logical	f	enthusiastic
c	caring	g	practical
d	thoughtful	h	inventive

3 Key

a	luck	b	honest	c	realistic

4 Key

a	stroke	d	with	g	beginner's
b	draw	e	no	h	push
c	out	f	take		

5 Key

1	behalf	6	with	11	comes
2	applied	7	serve	12	more
3	down	8	as	13	opinion/view
4	gets	9	times	14	hesitation
5	used	10	have		

Customs and traditions

Lead in p21

1 If you have a class with students from different countries, divide them into pairs or small groups to talk about festivals or celebrations from different places. Get feedback from individual students and ask if they were surprised by anything their partner(s) told them. Ask students from the same country to think of different regional festivals or celebrations.

2 Encourage students to compare and contrast the photos as in Part 2 Paper 5. Ask them to speculate about what they can see or what might be happening. Give some examples if necessary, e.g. *It looks like a cat. Maybe all the people dress up as animals. They might be having some kind of a fight. They seem to be throwing fruit or vegetables,* etc.

Background information

Kattenwoensdog
'Cat Wednesday' was introduced over two centuries ago in Ypres, Belgium, and is celebrated on the second Sunday of May. Traditionally the town jester threw cats from the belfry of the Cloth Hall but nowadays the cats are simply toys.

La Tomatina
La Tomatina is held every year in August in the town of Buñol, near Valencia. It had its origins in the 1940s when, it is said, a group of friends had an impromptu fight with tomatoes. Passers-by joined in and the weekly celebration now includes music, fireworks, food and general fun. Up to 20,000 combatants attend it every year.

3 Give students time to read through the questions and options first. Check they understand the meaning of *breed, rid the town of rodents, jester, crushed.*

Key

1 c 2 b 3 b 4 c

Tapescript 1

Last year, I travelled to Ypres in Belgium to pay a visit to the famous Cat Festival, which is held there on the second Sunday in May. 'Kattenwoensdog', which translates as 'Cat Wednesday', was introduced over two centuries ago. The story behind the festival is an interesting one. At that time, Ypres was an important centre for the wool trade. The wool was collected together in the town's huge Cloth Hall before it was sold. It attracted a lot of hungry rodents, so cats were used to control their numbers. **The cats subsequently bred and eventually became a nuisance and had to be got rid of.** Nowadays, the cats used in the festival are toys and the event is enhanced by parades celebrating famous cats. The festival was well worth the visit. It was extremely colourful and there was a fantastic atmosphere. What particularly attracted me was the parade of bands and beautifully decorated carnival floats – with so many different themes – which passed through the town. This was followed later on by a magnificent firework display on the town ramparts. But before that (**it had unfortunately started to rain by then but it didn't seem to make any difference to the spectators**), a jester appeared on the Cloth Hall tower and began to toss toy cats to the crowd below. Everyone scrambled to pick them up as a souvenir but I decided it would be much safer to buy one later at the tourist office to remind me of the event!

Tapescript 2

I was working in Valencia when a friend told me about a festival called La Tomatina. Apparently it has its origins in the 1940s, when a group of friends started an impromptu fight with some tomatoes. Passers-by joined in and the fiesta has continued to grow ever since. When my friend told me that you can expect upwards of 20,000 combatants to take part – double the town's population – I decided that this was something I had to see. I quickly found out that there are no alliances at La Tomatina – it's just the biggest food fight in the world. **The only rules are that you must squash the tomatoes in your hand before you throw them** and, if you can, hit a tourist – especially one with a camera. The ammunition was delivered to the square in the back of trucks to the accompaniment of the cheering crowds who'd been gathering since early morning. Once the signal had been given for hostilities to commence, it took just 30 minutes, and a lot of screaming, for 45,000 kilos of tomatoes to become a sticky, slimy mush. By the time it was all over, the streets were running red with tomato juice and we all looked like extras from a particularly violent movie. Luckily, **the town put up temporary public showers near the river so that we could rinse off the debris**. It was certainly an experience to remember!

4 You may want to give students a model before they talk. Write some key words or expressions about a festival you remember on the board (e.g. date/time of year, place, chain of events, etc.) and encourage students to ask you questions in order to build up a picture of your chosen festival. Suggest they think of questions to ask each other when describing their festival, e.g.: *Does it take place every year? How many people usually go?* etc. Get feedback from students and ask them to decide on the most unusual/interesting festivals, giving reasons why.

Reading p22

1 If students haven't been to any music festivals ask them about the kind of music they like/dislike and how important music is to them in general.

2 Refer students to the *How to do it* box. Remind them not to get distracted by vocabulary which they don't completely understand. Establish that the main idea of the first paragraph relates to travelling/ways of getting to the festival. Tell students to scan paragraphs A–G to find which one continues the theme of travel. Encourage them to underline words and phrases in the paragraph which link to the first paragraph of the main text. Tell them also to look particularly at the italicised phrase *a more appropriate form of transport* (l. 13) and to find a connection in one of paragraphs A–G (*in the vehicle* l. 105). If necessary, ask students the following questions to check they have understood the connection between the two sections of the text: *Why did the tourists sleep in their jeep?* (because it broke down and they were afraid to walk in the desert) *How do the Tuareg travel in the desert?* (on camels) *Which is the better means of transport?* (the camels are more appropriate).

Tell students to follow the same procedure with the remaining gaps, paying careful attention to the words and phrases in italics in the main text and paragraphs A–G. Tell them to note down any words and expressions with a similar meaning, e.g. *get-*

together (l. 17) *meeting* (l. 84), *little sign of sponsorship or the profit motive* (l. 37–38) *lack of commercialism* (l. 73).

Key

1 E   2 C   3 G   4 B   5 F   6 A
Paragraph D is not needed.

Background information

The Tuareg people are a nomadic tribe, mainly from the northern region of the Sahara desert. They are often known as 'the blue men of the desert' because of the indigo blue cloth they wear. They live in small tribes of up to 100 members and keep camels, chickens and goats. Drought and government policy have recently been threatening their traditional way of life.

3 Refer students back to the main text and paragraphs A–G to find examples of the phrases.

Key

a 5   b 2   c 4   d 7   e 8   f 6   g 1   h 3
To rephrase the sentences students may need to restructure just the phrase in italics or sometimes the whole sentence.

Suggested answers

a There is some doubt whether the festival will remain authentic.
b We sat at the back of the crowd but could just hear the music.
c There was a long delay before the concert began and people got very angry.
d As the bands began to play, we all got very excited along with everyone else.
e One old lady's reaction showed clearly that she (really) didn't like rock music (at all).
f The festival only started a few years ago so it's still quite new.
g Traditional music is one of the main things that attracts people/visitors to the country.
h There are few concerns about the effect the festival might have on the environment/ surroundings.

4 Suggested answers
Positive
- Cash spent by tourists can have a positive effect on the local economy.
- Local trade improves, and traditional handicrafts and music are promoted.

- The community is less isolated and has the chance to interact with the outside world.
- These improvement all have the effect of eliminating poverty and encouraging development.

Negative
- There is a danger that festivals like these will be taken over by big commercial interests.
- If only certain areas or communities are favoured, this might cause conflict.
- If this type of festival gets bigger, there could be negative environmental consequences

Vocabulary p24

1 Encourage students to keep organised records of collocations. Remind them that checking in a dictionary can help them select the correct collocation.

Key

a	made	d	told	g	have
b	keep	e	sets	h	earn
c	throw	f	jumped		

Optional activity

Where possible, students try to think of nouns which collocate with the other verbs in exercise 1. Use dictionaries if necessary. Make a class list. Divide the class into small groups and ask them to write sentences to illustrate their meaning in context.

2 Ask students what types of information can be found in dictionary entries, e.g. pronunciation, part of speech, structural patterns, examples. At CAE level, candidates should show high lexical accuracy, so encourage them to use dictionaries to find the most accurate collocations.

Key

bitterly disappointed
a highly   b immediately   c total

3 **Key**
a jump   b make   c kept

Grammar p24

1 Suggest students work in pairs/small groups to put the verbs under the correct headings in each column before referring to the grammar reference to check their answers.

Key

followed by a gerund	followed by an infinitive + *to*	followed by a gerund or infinitive
avoid	expect	like
enjoy	offer	prefer
practise	refuse	begin
fancy	want	continue
deny	threaten	love
miss	deserve	
risk	manage	
	hope	
	promise	

2 **Key**
expect   threaten   deny   hope   promise

3 **Key**

a	to win	e	to play/perform/appear
b	taking	f	seeing
c	to get	g	to be/arrive
d	to start	h	to arrest/shoot

Optional activity

Ask students to complete the following sentences with a gerund or infinitive form in a way which is true/appropriate for them. Students then compare their sentences in pairs/small groups.

a Next year, I hope ... (*to finish my university degree*)
b I always expect friends ...
c I would never risk ...
d In 10 years' time, I expect ...
e If I went to live in another country, I would probably miss ...

4 **Key**

a	try (doing)	f	mean (doing)
b	regret (doing)	g	regret (to do)
c	mean (to do)	h	stop (to do)
d	remember (to do)	i	remember (doing)
e	stop (doing)	j	try (to do)

Optional activity

Ask students to give example sentences for each of a–j.

Suggested answers

a I tried cooking using a wok to see if it was tastier.
b We regret having told her the truth.
c I mean to study harder for my next exams.
d She remembered to switch off the computer before she left.
e We stopped playing tennis when it started raining.
f The new law means having to wear a seatbelt at all-times.
g I regret to inform you that you have been unsuccessful.
h After working for five hours, they stopped to have a break.
i I remember giving you the key.
j We're trying to get through but all the lines are engaged.

5 After they have done this exercise individually, tell students to compare their answers in pairs. Get feedback from the whole class and correct any sentences which aren't clear.

Suggested answers

a I didn't remember inviting my neighbour to my barbecue so was surprised when he turned up.
I didn't remember to invite my neighbour to my barbecue and now he's not speaking to me.

b I wish for once you'd stop thinking about your problems.
I wish for once you'd stop to think before you act.

c I like our neighbours, but I regret saying that they could borrow our car.
I like our neighbours but I regret to say that they're very noisy at times.

d My six-month-old nephew has just tried eating chicken for the first time.
My six-month-old nephew has just tried to eat the whole birthday cake so he's been sick!

e Joining the army meant getting my hair cut.
Before I went on holiday I meant to get my hair cut.

6 Remind students that the gerund normally follows verb and preposition combinations. Tell them to try to choose the correct dependent preposition before completing the sentence with an appropriate verb in the gerund form.

Suggested answers

a keen on sailing
b to leaving
c in getting
d for leaving/keeping
e on getting/buying
f on talking/gossiping
g at writing
h of working

7 Refer students to the Grammar Reference to check their answers. In c), draw attention to the fact that *to* is necessary in the first part of the the sentence because the structure is passive, i.e. *make someone do something* but *be made to do something*.

Key

a ✓
b let that boy do
c make someone do
d ✓
e ✓
f better not tell
g watching you do something

8 You might want to give an example sentence first, e.g. *When I was a child my parents wouldn't let me eat junk food.*

Suggested answers

a … me eat junk food.
b … us to buy bottled water.
c … her leave the house.
d … stay at home tonight than go to the party.
e … the sun set.

9 After students have completed the exercise, ask them if they've ever done anything as adventurous or would like to do something similar.

Key

1	to do	8	being
2	to join	9	to burn
3	to think	10	to avoid
4	exploring	11	catch
5	discovering	12	seeing
6	to film	13	to go back
7	struggling		

Listening p26

1 Ask students to name any other groups which have had problems preserving their identity and culture, e.g. Australian aboriginals (see Background information below). Ask them to discuss which of the aspects mentioned in the quote they consider to be most important for preserving identity: history, land, language or values for younger generations. Encourage them to give reasons for their answers.

Background information

Native Americans had reached America thousands of years before the Europeans 'discovered' America in 1492. In the second half of the nineteenth century the American government herded them into reservations. The National Museum of the American Indian was established in 1989 in order to work with native peoples to protect and promote their cultures, traditions and beliefs.

2 Use the *tip* box to explain to students that the extracts are linked by theme, but there is no direct relationship between one extract and another. Before listening, ask students to read carefully through the questions for each extract and then check the *How to do it* box. Encourage students to write down any words or expressions they hear which helps to justify their answer, e.g. Extract 1, 1C: *should have been created long ago*.

Key

1 C   2 B   3 B   4 C   5 C   6 A

Tapescript

Extract 1
A: So, what can a tourist expect from your tours?
B: A real busy day! One of our most popular is the Museum of the Native American. Did you know that exhibits there were put together with collaboration from twenty-four different tribes and native communities? **And I have to say, a museum like this should have been created long ago to recognise the contributions native people have made to contemporary American culture and art.** And judging by the number of tourists, people agree with me!
A: But I suppose a museum like this takes a long time to set up?
B: That's true. I believe it started back in the early 1990s, when talks began with native communities. And this led to the museum's charter.

A: Which is … ?
B: It's called 'The Way of the People' and that should give you a clue. It represents the involvement of these different communities. **It's not just about exhibits; it's about actively showing visitors how the Native Americans lead their lives** through the recreation of different environments – a forest, a cropland …

Extract 2
A: Did you read what the newspaper said about that town fair we went to?
B: Didn't it say it was the largest one in its history? Nearly two thousand people or something? I remember when it was quite small!
A: Me too! But **apparently people travel from all over now and it's attracting a lot of publicity. It was certainly very busy** and the atmosphere – wonderful!
B: Yes, it was quite a day. I think what I enjoyed most was the beginning, you know, the procession through the town at midday, finishing up in the town square, with the musicians and dancers. And then there was that fantastic concert in the evening.
A: Not quite my cup of tea, but the fairground … There were so many different rides – great fun for the kids … and the adults. And those stalls selling local crafts, and the food stalls, were excellent value for money.
B: I think what really impressed me is that **all the money raised goes straight back to charities in the town or the area.**
A: Absolutely. It's a win-win situation for everyone!

Extract 3
A: One question I'd put to you is why artefacts of national importance should be housed in other countries. There are people (myself included) who would argue that they should be returned to their country of origin.
B: **I think that's a rather short-sighted view. If that were to happen, we would only ever learn about our own history – we'd become insular and less able to understand other nationalities and cultures.**
A: But what if that country wants them back?
B: In some cases it might be the right thing to do. But, let's face it, if this became a general policy many of the world's museums would be empty – hardly an encouragement for anyone to go to them.
A: So how do you view your role as a museum curator?
B: I think I've always looked upon it as a means of bringing the past alive. It's all too easy to regard history as being something in a text book. **What we need to do is make people aware not only of their own roots, but of all those people who inhabited the world long before we did.**

For extra practice with dictionaries and Listening, Part 1, see Worksheet 3 in the *Using a dictionary for exams* booklet in the Teacher's Pack.

Speaking p27

1 Explain to students that in Paper 5 Part 2, they will be asked to compare two photos in about a minute. It's important that they don't simply describe what they can see, but hypothesise about the photos and look for comparisons between them. After students have answered the questions, find out if any of them have seen/been to the types of ceremonies represented and ask them how they felt.

Key

a a graduation ceremony (1); the Olympic Games opening ceremony (2); a Remembrance Day parade (3)

Suggested answers

b They are usually quite formal; people wear special clothes or uniforms; there is a strict order of events; there is often music involved; they can be very emotional occasions.

c excited/elated/proud (1); thrilled/delighted/ nervous (2); nostalgic/tearful (3)

2 Remind students that even if they are nervous on the day of the exam and don't hear the examiner's instructions, they can follow the written prompts to complete the task. They have to focus on two issues here: how the people may be feeling, and how memorable the occasions might be.

3 Ask students if the candidate used any of the adjectives that they thought of in exercise 1.

Key

a proud/nervous/apprehensive/emotional
b She talks about how the people might be feeling but doesn't answer 'how memorable you think these occasions might be for them'. A closure technique is used when she cannot think of anything else to say (because she has not addressed the second part of the question) and this cuts the answer short.

Tapescript

Candidate: Well, in this the students are getting a degree. They're proud, that's sure. Yes, proud. And in this picture this person I think is nervous – yes, maybe nervous that something might go wrong. This picture looks as if it's the Olympic Games ceremony – yes, it's the Olympic Games. Well, these people might be feeling apprehensive about whether they are going to win or lose. But they might also be feeling emotional because they are taking part in such a wonderful ceremony. Well, … that's all, I think!

4 Draw students' attention to some of the useful structures used in the sentences, e.g. *It looks as if/appear to be/think … would be/you would probably,* etc. These are helpful when speculating or hypothesising. Remind them of the difference between *take place* (used to talk about events happening) and *take part in* (used to talk about people participating in something), and between *remember* and *remind*. The comparative structure *more … than* should help them with d).

Key

a 7 b 8 c 2 d 1 e 4 f 3 g 5 h 6

5 Set a time limit of about one minute per student.

There is authentic practice of this section on page 92 of the Workbook.

Use of English p28

1 If students have difficulty understanding the phrase *coming of age*, explain that it indicates the time when someone gets the rights and responsibilities of an adult.

2 Key
a They are a Brazilian Amazon tribe.
b Young men aged 14–18.

3 Refer students to the *How to do it* box. Ask them to look carefully at what part of speech is missing. Remind students that the words are usually short, for example, prepositions, linking words, auxiliary verbs, pronouns, etc. Suggest students check their answers using the information in the *tip* box.

Key

1	One	6	because	11	When/Once
2	order	7	come	12	to/towards
3	This/It	8	For/Over	13	as
4	that/which	9	who	14	in/near
5	with	10	being	15	their

5 Explain to students that the objective is to transform information from one sentence to another without changing the meaning. Remind students they can't change the key word given. Point out how the lexis and grammar changes, but not the meaning, in the example sentence.

Key

Do you think I could   Yes

6 Refer students to the *How to do it* box. Remind them to look carefully at the tenses and form in the first sentence before deciding which are correct or not.

Key

a is the actor whose autobiography came
b not have to put up with
c correct
d far less painful
e if the result will be

For extra practice with dictionaries and Use of English, Part 5 see Worksheet 9 in the *Using a dictionary for exams* booklet in the Teacher's Pack.

Grammar p29

1 Before students do the exercises remind them of the differences between defining and non-defining relative clauses and refer back to the clauses on page 28 for examples.

Key

a 9 b 7 c 8 d 2 e 5 f 1 g 4 h 6 i 10 j 3

Writing p30

1 If any students have been to Australia, ask them to tell the class about what they remember about their stay there. Ask students what impression they have of life in Australia and how it compares to their own culture and what would be equivalent pictures from their own culture.

Key

a Australia
b music, the arts and entertainment (the Sydney Opera house/Kylie Minogue), sports (surfing), native peoples (Uluru/Ayers Rock, Aboriginal with boomerang), famous sites (Uluru)

Background information

Australia is an island continent whose climate ranges from tropical rain forests to deserts and snow-covered mountains. Before European settlers arrived in 1788 it was inhabited by indigenous people who today make up about 4% of the population. The first migrants were mainly English convicts but the gold rush years (1800's) attracted immigrants from Britain, Ireland, Germany and China. There was large scale migration after the Second World War and people from around 200 countries have migrated to Australia.

2 Remind students of the importance of reading the question carefully and responding accurately to it. Suggest they underline the key words before answering a–c.

Key

a the festival organiser
b a proposal
c what should be included in the festival and why you think the aspects you have chosen would be of interest.

3 Key

a F   d T   f F
b T   e T   g T
c F

4 Ask students if they think the ways of showing the ideas are suitable or if they can think of other ideas.

Key

a photographic display, a procession, a video, photos, food-tasting stall, live performance, stills from films

5 Key

a show/to show
b teach/teaching/that we teach
c invite/to invite
d put on/us to put on

Other ways of making suggestions:
Visitors might also enjoy …
We could follow that …
We could also have …
Visitors would be amazed by …
We could include …
Another aspect that would interest visitors …

6 Make sure students are aware that the expressions in the model are more suitable because the style is more formal and the vocabulary chosen is more sophisticated.

Key

a their culture is completely unique
b a procession of historic characters
c bring our history alive
d Visitors would be amazed and captivated … by the wildlife
e Kylie Minogue … would be an obvious choice

7 Suggest that students give a heading for their proposal, e.g. *Proposal for the International Cultural Festival in London*.

For an assessed authentic answer to this Writing task, see page 7 of the *Writing and Speaking Assessment Booklet* in the Teacher's Pack.

Review p32

1 Key

a Parades are public processions.
b Traditions are customs and beliefs handed down to future generations.
c Rituals are a prescribed order of performing rites.
d Ceremonies are formal public occasions.
e Festivals are days or periods of celebration.

2 Key

a has been called into question
b within earshot of
c to get caught up/to get swept up

3 Key

a earn   e deeply
b sets   f breaking
c fiercely   g absolutely
d passionately h bitterly

4 Key

a contribution   d requirements
b carving   e formation
c revelation   f recognition

5 Key

a memorable   c reminded   e forget
b memories   d unforgettable

6 Key

a 2   b 4   c 3   d 5   e 1

Looking ahead

Lead in p33

1 Suggested answers

a The photos show birds migrating, a horse race about to start, a graph showing the rise and fall of share prices, berries, a microscope, and a tropical storm. These show situations in which people make predictions relating to gambling and betting on sport, finance, a good or bad harvest of crops or perhaps predictions of the weather ahead based on natural signs, scientific development and perhaps the development of diseases, and weather events and the environment.

b Mainly jobs related to the fields of medicine, the environment, scientific research, and economic growth. Examples include doctors, weather forecasters, economists and business analysts, and sports pundits.

c In many instances, the general public but also specific jobs, e.g. farmers depend on accurate weather forecasting.

d This depends on the situation and whether the prediction was positive or negative but there could be economic, medical and environmental effects to smaller or larger degrees.

2 Before students work in pairs or small groups to answer the question, tell them to look at the expressions for *Making predictions* and decide whether they refer to things that are likely to happen/unlikely to happen, etc. Encourage students to use the expressions when doing the exercise. Set a time limit of about four minutes so that students get used to the timing for Paper 5 Part 3.

Reading p34

1 Remind students that in Part 1 of the Reading the extracts are linked by a theme, but there is no direct relationship between them. Ask students to look at the first few lines of each extract quickly and say what aspects of the future they deal with (space travel, the Internet and business, technological advances). Then ask students to read the extracts quickly and write a title for each one. Ask them to tell the class their ideas.

2 Refer students to the *How to do it* box. Remind them to read the questions and options carefully before making their final choice. Ask students to make a note of where they found the information in the extract to justify their answers. You might want to set a time limit of twenty minutes to get students used to distributing their time effectively.

Key

1 D   2 B   3 B   4 C   5 A   6 C

Optional activity

Students work in small groups to discuss the advantages or disadvantages of each development and compare their opinions with those expressed by the writers.

If you prefer to divide up the extracts between students and have them exchange ideas, give each student round the class an extract to read and answer. Divide the class up into those who read extract 1, 2 or 3 to check and compare their answers. Student then re-form into groups of three (extract 1, 2, 3) and summarize the content, explaining their answers for each question.

For extra practice with dictionaries and Reading, Part 1 see Worksheet 3 in the *Using a dictionary for exams* booklet in the Teacher's Pack.

Vocabulary p36

1 Refer students to the Grammar Reference before they do the exercise. Ask them to find examples of phrasal verbs in the texts on pages 34 and 35 and to check their meaning, e.g. *sign up* (l. 9), *hooked up* (l. 24), *try on* (l. 46), *bring back* (l. 48).

Key

a   put up   d   broke up
b   set up   e   turn down
c   bring down

2 Key

a   all
b
b   His intention is to use the inheritance to set it up.
c   Protesters are threatening to bring them/it down.
d   Police broke it up by firing tear gas into the crowd.
e   It was the thought of commuting every day that made me turn it down.

3 Key

a   broke down
b   put your brother/him down
c   turn up
d   set down

For extra practice with dictionaries and phrasal verbs see Worksheet 8 in the *Using a dictionary for exams* booklet in the Teacher's Pack.

Grammar p36

1 Suggest students read the Grammar Reference before doing the exercises in this section or to check their answers against it afterwards.

Key

a   3   present simple
b   1   present continuous
c   4   future perfect simple
d   2   *will*
e   7   future continuous
f   6   *going to* + infinitive
g   5   future perfect continuous

2 Key

1   are going to get   4   I'll ring
2   is starting   5   is having
3   will go   6   they'll make

3 Point out the time phrases in each sentence:

a   by 2020
b   within the next five years
c   in the very near future
d   by next year
e   in 50 years' time

Key

a   will be working
b   Will ... have become
c   will be using
d   will have cloned
e   will be living

Note that the simple future form with *will* is also possible in all of these sentences.

5 Key

a   *as soon as* 2 (present perfect)
b   *when* 3 (present simple)
c   *while* 1 (present continuous)

6 Suggested answers

a   you get there/have arrived
b   you finish work/have had a rest
c   I have been to my pilates class/I eat a good meal.
d   you are 30/you've left college?
e   he has finished with the other customer/he is free.

They can all be followed by the present simple or present perfect.

7 Refer students to page 169 in the Grammar Reference: *The future in the past* before they do the exercise.

Key

a   was planning/had planned/had been planning
b   was to open/was going to open
c   was about to take
d   would/stay/be staying/was going to stay

8 Suggested answers

a when they realised neither of them had any money.
b when the phone rang.
c be ill today, I wouldn't have come into work.
d be unpopular with my friends.

9

You might want to use this exercise to give more practice of the second part of Paper 5 Part 1. Introduce it with 'Now I'd like you to ask each other … what you're doing for a holiday this year' and encourage students to rephrase questions a–e. Set a limit of 60–90 seconds for each question.

Listening p38

1

Ask students to name other similar places to the ones in the photos (Stonehenge and Petra), particularly ones in their own country. Encourage them to discuss how such places are preserved and what problems there may be (cost, environmental damage, vandalism, commercialisation, etc.).

Suggested answers

Limit the numbers of tourists visiting the monuments/sites, close the area to tourism at certain times of the year, charge higher entry prices and re-invest in conservation.

Background information

Stonehenge
Stonehenge, in the south of England, was built in several stages from 2800–1800 BC. It is thought to have been built to allow observation of astronomical phenomena.

Petra
Petra (meaning 'rock' in Greek) is in Jordan. It became important in the late first century BC due to the success of the spice trade.

2

Ask students to say whether Bob and Carrie make any of the suggestions they made themselves in exercise 1.

Key

1 C 2 D 3 B 4 A 5 C 6 D

Tapescript

Interviewer: There's a lot of discussion nowadays about what lies in store for old buildings and monuments. Now you're both involved in looking after places like these. Bob, what do you think is the best way of going about this so they don't suffer unduly from the rising numbers of tourists visiting them?

Bob: Well, one of the ways that you can do this is to build a tourist centre. About 13 years ago a firm of architects won a competition to design a new tourist centre for one of Britain's most prestigious ancient monuments – Stonehenge. There's no shortage of financial backing but the centre is still in the pipeline and **the debate over what exactly it should offer visitors thunders on.** Most people, and that includes me, start to ask themselves 'Who is it for? How accessible should it be? Will it simply encourage-even more visitors to come to the site?' and so on.

Carrie: Indeed. Personally, I feel we should do something quite dramatic, like forget the whole thing, close all the existing visitor facilities at Stonehenge and remove any references to those famous standing stones from all the tourist literature. In other words, **leave the place alone for anyone who happens to come along to discover it for the first time**, as it were.

Bob: Great plan but totally unrealistic, of course, and Carrie knows that only too well. That's because **the tourist industry is an invaluable revenue earner**, so there's no way that's ever going to happen – everyone's well aware that some kind of money-spinning centre is on the cards. The point is that Stonehenge is one of those sites that just has to be visited. Petra is another. The rose-red city is one of the world's most alluring tourist sites. It's a truly magical place.

Carrie: It certainly is, and so of course is Stonehenge. But apart from being a must for travellers, there are so many other similarities between the two sites. One of the most significant, in my opinion, is that they could both be overwhelmed by visitors in the future. There are plans to build a tourist centre at Petra, too – a five million dollar visitor and interpretation centre. The project's been controversial but what they're going to try and do is **tuck the centre into the surrounding hills.** Apparently it won't dominate the entrance to Petra. It will lead visitors gently in and out of the site without in any way damaging it.

Bob: I agree that the Petra project certainly is an impressive one but what appeals to me most about it is the fact that it'll offer tourists a more in-depth look at the site. Too many tourists arrive at a place of interest, pay their sometimes exorbitant entrance fee, then make a dash for the main attractions. They often miss out on the carefully thought-out displays designed to give them **an idea of why the place was built, what role it had in history, what kind of people lived there, what their daily life was like.**

Carrie: I hope it succeeds in getting that message across to visitors, but from what I've read about the project, the aim seems to be to **maintain the aura of Petra as a lost city, a place to be discovered. Again, it's a bit like Stonehenge in this respect, and the people I've talked to about the plans for Petra certainly feel that it should reveal its secrets slowly,** rather than all at once, to its numerous visitors. It should keep that vital element of dramatic surprise so that the visitor never knows what's round the corner. I think if the project manages to achieve that, despite all the publicity surrounding it, and ensures that the vast numbers of tourists don't damage it for ever, it will have been very successful indeed.

Bob: Absolutely. It would certainly be a tragedy if places like these weren't protected in some way and I suppose I have to admit that building something like a visitor centre is one way of ensuring that places like these do survive intact. And in the long run, it's up to every one of us to make sure that they do.

Interviewer: Bob, Carrie, thanks for sharing your views with us this evening …

3 Key

a 2   b 4   c 1   d 5   e 3

Speaking p39

1 If you have students of different age groups, put different ages into pairs or small groups to see if their ambitions are significantly different. Take class feedback.

2 Key
Success: a, d, e, f
Failure: b, i
Making an effort: c, g, h, j

Ask students to suggest more expressions for the different headings, e.g. success: *be a hit*, failure: *be a flop/not be up to something*, making an effort: *have a go at something*.

3 Ask students to say what types of ambition are represented in the photos, e.g. winning a sports competition, designing something for the world of fashion. Focus attention on the task above the photos while they make notes.

4 Suggested answer
The candidate doesn't compare the photos. He tends to repeat himself and doesn't use a range of structures or vocabulary or expand on his ideas.

Tapescript

I'm going to choose this picture of singers and this one here of the runner. In this picture there are young people. They're singing – maybe at school. I think they might want to be singers. I don't think this is difficult. In fact it might be quite easy for them to do this. In the other picture, I can see a girl in a race – perhaps in a stadium. Maybe she wants to be an athlete. She can be, I think. It's possible. Anything's possible.

5 Remind students they only have about 30 seconds to answer the follow-up task, so they need to be brief and precise.

Suggested answer

I think she hasn't described the picture of the man designing something or the picture of the woman fitting the clothes on a model.

6 Make sure students try to do the task within the required time limit (about a minute for the photos and approximately 30 seconds for the follow up question.) Students could work in threes and take turns in the role of the examiner.

Use of English p40

1 You could also ask students at what stage of life your age is more obvious, and whether it's easier to tell the age of men or women. If you have a mixture of nationalities/cultures in class you could extend the discussion to include the following: 'To what extent is your culture 'ageist'? How respected are older people in your society?' With a younger class, find out if they have grandparents and what kind of relationship they have with them, and whether they consider them 'old' or not.

Suggested answer

You can probably guess someone's age to within five years – it's generally easier to tell the age of children and babies more accurately and probably more difficult as people get older. Factors that may give clues to someone's age are the way they dress, the kind of language and expressions they use, their interests, perhaps what their taste in music is, etc.

2 Key

Your calendar age is based on your date of birth. Your biological age reflects your health, fitness, lifestyle and family medical history.

3 As well as following the advice in the *Tip* box, students could read the text to predict what part of speech might fit in each gap. Remind them that it is a good idea to keep a record of verbs followed by dependent prepositions.

Key

1 A   2 D   3 B   4 D   5 B   6 A   7 C   8 D   9 B
10 C   11 A   12 B

Optional activity

In groups ask students to choose two or three of the options in 1–15, check the meaning of any words they don't understand in a dictionary and then write sentences to illustrate the meaning of each word. Monitor and check that students are aware of any dependent prepositions or if any of the words cause confusion,e.g. *argues/discusses*. Students pass their sentences to other groups to check or correct.

For extra practice with dictionaries and Use of English, Part 1 see Worksheet 7 in the *Using a dictionary for exams* booklet in the Teacher's Pack.

4 Put students into small groups to try the different tests. Ask them to invent one more to try out on a different group. All the tests are related to physical agility, so they might want to try to invent something which tests, for example, memory.

Vocabulary p41

1 Encourage students to check their answers in a dictionary after they have completed the exercise.

Key

a 8   b 1   c 6   d 2   e 5   f 7   g 3   h 4

2 You could extend the discussion by asking the following questions:
- Is there an ideal age?
- What are the things you like/dislike about your present age?
- How have things changed for you since you were a-child?
- What are some of the advantages of getting older?

Writing p42

1 Remind students to always read the exam question carefully and underline key words so that they are sure what they are writing, to whom and for what purpose. This will help them decide on the appropriate layout and register.

Key

a He is planning to open the university car park to the general public and charge students for parking facilities, and also stop the free bus service for students.

b The Principal, P. Simpson.

2 Key

a appropriate (formal and we know the name of the person to write to)

b inappropriate (direct questions can be too informal and the phrase *how on earth* is rather rude)

c appropriate

d inappropriate (*Hi* is too informal)

e inappropriate (*For a start* and *just plain wrong* sound rather aggressive and too informal)

f appropriate

g inappropriate (*It's crazy* and *awful* sound too informal and rather rude)

3 Suggested answers

a We have recently carried out a survey.

b This information is incorrect.

c The changes you would like to implement.

d We cannot support this motion/decision.

e This is discriminatory.

Optional activity

After students have completed the task, ask them to rewrite the inappropriate sentences in 2 (b, d, e, g) in a more suitable formal style as well.

Suggested answers

b If the general public is permitted to use the car park facilities, students will have difficulty finding spaces.

d Dear Mr. Simpson

e Firstly, your conclusions about students use of the bus services are incorrect.

g In our opinion, it is not very realistic to expect students to cycle to college considering the traffic problems in our city.

---

4 Suggested answers

1 these are under-used: According to our student survey 58% of students use the free buses or the student car park more than three times a week.

2 The free buses run half empty: These are used to the maximum by students during the winter months.

3 make the car park available to the general public: In our opinion, there is already a lack of parking space during the day.

4 Students will also be required to pay these parking charges: It is not very likely that, on a student budget, we will be able to afford the parking fees.

5 encourage students to cycle to college: In our opinion, it is not very realistic to expect students to cycle to college considering the traffic problems in our city.

6 I trust the committee will support our decision: It seems only fair that you reconsider your proposal based on our comments.

5 Encourage students to share ideas. Check that they use the linking words in the correct position and include commas where necessary.

Suggested answers

1 You point out that the college has run into debt. *However,* we were unaware of this problem.

2 You mention that the parking facitities are underused. *Nevertheless,* according to our survey, 58% of students use the free buses or the student car park more than three times a week.

3 You note that the free buses run half empty, *although* in fact these are used to the maximum by students during the winter months.

4 You suggest students will be required to pay these parking charges *in spite of/despite* the fact that it is not very likely that, on a student budget, we will be able to afford the parking fees.

5 You suggest encouraging students to cycle to college, but, in our opinion, this is not very realistic *because of* the traffic problems in our city.

6 Suggested answer

Dear Mr Simpson

I am writing on behalf of the student committee in response to your recent memo regarding financial cutbacks at the college. In your memo, you state that the transport services are used by an insufficient number of students. However, this is not in fact the case. May I draw your attention to the fact that a majority of students use one or other of the services more than once a week. Although the buses may not be filled to capacity during the summer, in winter they are full.

As regards the car park and the proposed changes you plan to introduce, I fear these are also unacceptable. While allowing outsiders to use the car park may seem advantageous, it would actually mean fewer parking spaces for students. As for parking charges, we believe it is totally unjust to expect students to pay for their own facilities. It is also a fact that many students do not have sufficient money to afford such a fee. Coming to college by bicycle is, sadly, not an option as the level of traffic in the city makes cycling much too risky a venture.

Given all the points above, I have to inform you that after careful consideration we have decided to oppose these drastic measures.

Yours sincerely

For an assessed authentic answer to this Writing task, see page 8 of the *Writing and Speaking Assessment Booklet* in the Teacher's Pack.

Review p44

1 Key

a	broke down	e	put someone down
b	set up	f	sets down
c	put some up	g	break up
d	brought up		

2 Key

a	around the	c	in the long	e	on the
b	in the	d	was in		

3 Key

a	giving	e	making
b	beat	f	heart and soul
c	make	g	make
d	lacked	h	come up with

4 Key

a	based	c	interest	e	trade
b	enquire	d	addition	f	unless

5 Key

a	getting	d	shoulders	f	look
b	heart	e	better	g	hills
c	feel				

6 Key

1 e 2 g 3 b 4 a 5 f 6 d 7 c

Into the wild

Lead in p45

1 Suggested answers

1 mane: horse, lion
2 flipper: dolphin, turtle
3 fin: shark, goldfish
4 wing: any bird, bee
5 scale: any fish, snake
6 antenna: butterfly, moth
7 claw: cat, lion, tiger
8 shell: snail, tortoise
9 beak: any bird
10 hoof: cow, horse
11 horn : bull, goat
12 hide: elephant, rhinoceros
13 tusk: elephant, walrus
14 paw: dog, rabbit

2 Put students into groups to compare their ideas.

Suggested answers

a spider, snake, shark, scorpion
b cockroach, toad, slug
c monkey, gorilla
d domesticated animals such as cats, dogs and those kept as pets, e.g. hamsters, rabbits, etc. and possibly animals such as donkeys, horses, etc. used for work
e shark, black widow spider (the female eats the male), scorpion, bat
f tiger, tropical fish
g great white shark, Asian elephant, tiger

3 Key

a primates, e.g. monkey, baboon
   agile means *flexible, supple, fast*; *sociable* means *friendly and living in groups*; *grooming* means *cleaning*
b dolphin
   intelligent means *clever*
c giraffe
   graceful means *elegant*
d cheetah
   fierce means *cruel and vicious*
   stalk their prey means *hunt their victims*

4 You could ask students to include one creature that is generally feared, one which is exotic and one which is endangered.

Reading p46

1 Students may be able to give personal accounts or think of films or books or stories in the news.

2 Suggested answer

People have long believed that dolphins are more intelligent and possibly kinder than other animals, and there are a number of stories of them 'helping' humans. However, some scientists believe that, like all species, they may only have been acting out of self-interest.

After students have done the exercise check the meaning of any difficult vocabulary, e.g. *kinship* (l.-35), *altruism* (l.-61).

3 Elicit from students that l. 1–8 and 9–12 describe a particular incident and therefore the missing paragraph is likely to give more information about this (c). Tell them to read missing paragraphs A–G and to first identify the paragraph describing what led up to the situation (G). In pairs they then match a) and b) with other paragraphs.

Key

The first missing paragraph will describe what led up to this situation (c).
a C   b A   c G

4 Key

1 G   2 E   3 C   4 B   5 A   6 D
Paragraph F is not needed.

5 Explain to students this is a useful exercise for double-checking their answers.

Suggested answers

2 *great white shark* (l. 12) is a *fearsome predator* (l. 65)
3 *believed* (l. 18) links to *Such a belief* (l. 57).
4 *Such questions* (l. 27) picks up on the questions asked in paragraph B.
5 *biologists have argued for years* (l. 28) is picked up by *The modern version of this debate* (l. 47)
6 The theory in lines 37–39 is picked up in *This may explain altruism* (l. 61), and the questions in paragraph D relate to *Whatever the answer* (l.-40).

For extra practice with dictionaries and Reading, Part 2, see Worksheet 3 in the *Using a dictionary for exams* booklet in the Teacher's Pack.

Vocabulary p48

1 Encourage students to check the meanings in a dictionary. Ask if they have similar expressions in their own language.

Key

a	time	c	bag	e	grass
b	dinner	d	water	f	work

2 Suggested answers

a can't stand it!
b will be doing the exam.
c he's hardly eaten a thing today.
d spilt coffee all over their new carpet.
e she's serious about getting married.

Grammar p48

1 Tell students to check their answers in the Grammar Reference.

Key

a past simple
b past perfect continuous
c present perfect simple
d past continuous
e present perfect simple
f present perfect simple
g past continuous
h past perfect simple
i present perfect continuous

2 Key

b	present perfect simple	e	past continuous
c	past perfect simple	f	present perfect
d	past perfect continuous		

3 Key

a I studied (*until*)
b have tasted (*first time*)
c excelled (*as a child*)
d I've twisted (the exclamation *Ouch!* indicates the action is very recent)
e dared (*before*)
f I've resisted (*for the past six weeks*)
g produced (Shakespeare is dead)

4 Key

a has played
b have been working
c have phoned
d have read
e has been travelling

5 Once students have written their sentences, ask them to compare them in pairs and encourage them to ask further questions, e.g. example (a) *Really? What was it about? Did many people go?*

6 Suggested answers

1 a The policeman saw the motorist and arrested him at that moment.

  b The motorist had broken the law before he was stopped. Arrested is the more recent of the two events.

2 a The fire bell interrupted the exam.

  b Most students had finished the exam when the fire bell rang.

7 Key

a had been crying   d landed/was landing
b killed   e was sitting
c was repairing   f hadn't plugged it in!

8 Key

1 have seen
2 have ever observed
3 have been fascinated
4 was
5 got
6 accompanied
7 had attacked
8 cut
9 followed
10 found
11 had been feeding/had fed
12 caught
13 were sitting
14 were playing
15 stared
16 scratched
17 yawned

9 Put students into small groups and check they are using a variety of tenses.

Listening p50

1 Suggested answers

Wildlife photographers film creatures, normally in the wild. They would need to be patient, have quick reactions, an understanding of the animals' behaviour, perhaps need to be physically fit and adventurous, have respect for the environment, etc.

2 Before students listen, tell them to read thorough the notes and see if they can correct any spelling mistakes or obviously wrong answers. Remind them that spelling must be correct to get maximum marks and that in sentence completion answers must fit grammatically. Predicting is also an important skill for Part 2 as candidates only hear the piece once.

Key

1 Amazon (*South Africa* wrong because not the most recent trip)
2 school leavers (only some comes from schoolchildren)
3 amateurs (*really good quality pictures* is too long and doesn't fit with operating)
4 teacher (*teaching* doesn't fit the grammatical context)
5 B/biology (*Biography* is a similar word but incorrect)
6 conservationist (*conversationist* is probably a spelling mistake)
7 enough money (*compensation* doesn't make sense and changes the form of the word – you should write what you hear)
8 B/business (the text says 'forget about creative subjects' so this is a distractor)

Tapescript

Good afternoon and welcome. I gather all of you are interested in becoming wildlife photographers, so I've brought along some of the pictures I took on two of my most interesting assignments. The first was to South Africa, where I went last year. It's probably one of the best places in the world to be if you're a wildlife photographer! And the second was on my most recent trip to **the Amazon**, where the wildlife is also amazing. I'll let you see these later, but first of all I'd like to tell you what being a wildlife photographer entails. Every day, I get emails from people asking me what they have to do to become a professional wildlife photographer. Some of these emails come from schoolchildren doing projects about a future career they would be interested in taking up. But **most of these requests come from school leavers** seriously thinking about a career as a wildlife photographer. Usually my first reaction is 'I don't know!' But of course this doesn't help. It does however indicate that there is no easy answer to this question. It is actually incredibly difficult to become more than a part-time freelancer. There are **so many amateurs flooding the market** with really good quality pictures that it's very hard to make a living from it. Most of the famous professionals in wildlife photography never had any formal training. Arthur Morris, probably the best known bird photographer, **had been a teacher** for years before going full-time into photography. I've only once met anyone with any kind of formal training. He attended a university in England where he did a degree in what's called **Biology**

Imaging, which also includes photography, filming and drawing. And he still ended up working as a safari guide! The best way to get yourself into the profession is to do it alongside a job that brings you as close as possible to your subjects. **This could be as a conservationist** or travel guide. Then while photographing, you can slowly start selling pictures while your experience and expertise grows. After a few years, you might decide that you can give up the other job. One thing many people overlook is that, once you are a professional, it's no longer about taking great pictures because you love it. **It's about earning enough money** to compensate for all the expenses such as equipment, films, processing, travel, etc. This puts quite a few people off. But you have to remember that you will not only be marketing your pictures, but, in a way, also yourself. So if you're wondering what subject would be best to take at university, **forget about creative subjects and take Business**. You'll certainly find it useful. Now, if you'd like to take a look at these pictures …

Speaking p50

1 Ask students to look briefly at the photos on page 51 and to identify the different animals. Find out if any students have any of these animals as pets and why they are important to them personally. Students should use the examiner's question to complete the missing information.

Key

1	important	4	situations
2	animals	5	two
3	people	6	best illustrate

2 Check students can pronounce the missing words correctly and know where the stress falls on each word. Put them into groups to share ideas and encourage them to expand on their answers as much as possible by giving explanations or examples.

Key

a 5   b 1   c 3   d 2   e 4

Suggested answers

a to patrol places like parks or green areas instead of using cars and are sometimes used to break up riots.

b find it comforting because it's said cats have a very calming effect on people's lives.

c to feed it and take care of it. Owning a pet can also be a good way of teaching young children about illness and death.

d you might not be able to get around so easily, and the dog can also become a much-loved friend.

e it's interesting to see them in a fairly natural habitat, and to be able to get so close to them.

3 Tell students to make a note of which candidate does or doesn't follow each piece of advice in the *How to do it* box.

Suggested answers

a She starts with the second part of the task first rather than talking about all the pictures first.

b He redirects the task at the beginning and tries to expand on his ideas as much as possible.

c He interrupts his partner constantly and dominates the conversation.

Tapescript

Female: So we have to choose two pictures to illustrate the website article. I think these two are the best. What about you?

Male: I think we should talk about the pictures first. Let's begin with this one. Now it seems to be a walk-through aquarium – I think it's called a walk-through aquarium – and some children are visiting it.

Female: Yes I agree. But I think …

Male: No, wait a minute. It could be that it's a party of schoolchildren and it's an educational visit to find out about wildlife. It could be that the class is doing a project on marine life, or something like that. I think the fish might be really important in this situation. I mean the children couldn't do the project without actually going to see them.

Female: Maybe not, but what about the photo of the couple with the pet cat…

Male: Oh, the pet cat. Now that's a good picture to illustrate the importance of animals because pets make some people really happy. Some people would find it difficult to manage without them. Yes, that's definitely worth considering. But let's talk about the other pictures.

4 Ask students to think about ways of starting the activity as one of them will have to take the initiative at the beginning, e.g.

So, shall we start with this picture?
Right, what do you think about this one?

Ask students to each choose two or three different questions from the useful phrases section and to try to use them while they do the task. Set a time limit of up to four minutes. Monitor and check that both students are speaking and that one is not dominating the conversation.

Use of English p52

1 Before students discuss the pictures, focus on useful language for hypothesising and comparing. This is important for Paper 5 Part 2, e.g.

I think it might be/could be (a kind of giant turtle).
It looks like (an elephant).
It looks like as if (it's got giant wings).
It's more like a (dinosaur) *than a* (tortoise).
It's got (sharper teeth) *than* (the flying fish).

2 You could divide students into groups of four and ask them to read one short text each and then give feedback to their group. This will give further practice of the language practised in exercise 1. Ask them to justify their reasons based on the information in the text, e.g. *I think mine could be picture 2 because it says it can fly and swim.*

Key

a   Snowstalker (picture 3)
b   The Megasquid (picture 1)
c   The Toraton (picture 4)
d   The Ocean Flish (picture 2)

3 Check any unknown vocabulary before students do the exercise, e.g. (a) *ferocious, predator, blizzard, sturdy*; (b) *elongating, compressing*; (c) *humble, grazing, swamps, collides*.

Key

1	of	5	by	8	with
2	under	6	from	9	out
3	for	7	at	10	into
4	through				

4 Key

1   has (*be around* means exist. *Been* indicates the tense is present perfect simple.)
2   according
3   If
4   off
5   with
6   of
7   such
8   out
9   more
10   like
11   at
12   where
13   the
14   is
15   no

5 Tell students to work in pairs to write a short description of an imaginary creature. Refer them back to the texts on page 52 for ideas. Other classmates could try and guess the name of the animal from its characteristics, e.g. *Snagaroo* (snail + kangaroo), *Kangaraffe* (kangaroo + giraffe), *Chamopard* (chameleon + leopard).

Writing p54

1 If students are unfamiliar with the animals in the photos ask them to think of another animal which lives in the wild in their country and talk about it, using the same categories as prompts.

Key

wild boar, hedgehog, otter (p 54 clockwise from top), squirrel, bear, tortoise (p 55 left to right)

2 Remind students that they should always identify the key points in the exam question before planning their answer.

Key

one wild animal, your country, visitors … interested to see, details about the animal, advice on how to observe

3 Make sure students note the importance of giving a heading for each paragraph to divide the information clearly and to ensure they are answering both parts of the question. Check the meaning of any unknown vocabulary.

Key

a to clearly separate the two areas of information asked for

b appearance of body, diet, character/behaviour, habitat

c when: at night or early in the day if they live by the sea
where: by rivers or on the coast in Britain.
how: drive along the coast and sit quietly on the-beach

4 Key

a These attractive creatures live near rivers …
b As well as being skilful swimmers …
c Their homes are made from piles of branches …
d Catching sight of an otter … is quite a challenge-…
e Those that live by rivers are mostly nocturnal …
f The best place to see an otter in this country is on the west coast.

5 Encourage students to complete the sentences themselves before looking back at the text, as they may have different ideas.

Key

a adapted   d playful   f secretive
b on a   e solitary   g nocturnal
c fond

6 Key

a Finding an eagle's nest
b It's easy to
c Seeing a lion at close quarters
d Wearing bright colours

For an assessed authentic answer to this Writing task, see page 9 of the *Writing and Speaking Assessment Booklet* in the Teacher's Pack.

Review p56

1 Key

a 7, 9   b 2, 8, 10   c 3, 5   d 6, 11, 12   e 4   f 1

2 Key

1 hen party   4 rabbiting on
2 had butterflies   5 like a horse
3 in the doghouse

3 Key

a fish   b donkey   c whale   d dog's   e cat

4 Key

1 out   4 of   7 to
2 with   5 at   8 at
3 off   6 for

5 Suggested answer

Toucans can be found in South and Central America. Despite the fact that there are no wild specimens in the UK, you can see large numbers of them in zoos. These creatures are easily recognised by their sizeable, brightly coloured beaks, which are about half the size of their body. Particularly fond of fruit, seeds and insects, they are sociable creatures, given to staying in groups.

Health matters

Lead in p57

1 Ask students if they already do any of 1–10 and which they think are good or bad ideas.

2 Tell students to work in small groups to compare their ideas and choose the two best suggestions.

Suggested answers

Shopping: walk to the shops instead of driving whenever possible, and carry items home.

Housework: instead of getting a cleaner, try and do it yourself from time to time! It may involve stretching and bending as well as working arm/wrist muscles.

Getting ready for work/school: do some quick stretching excercises when you get out of bed in the morning, and eat a healthy breakfast to give you energy.

Getting around: walk or cycle whenever possible. If travelling by bus, get off one or two stops early and walk the rest of the way.

3 Encourage students to use appropriate language for making suggestions/recommendations, e.g. *ought to*, *should*, *it's a good idea to*, etc.

Suggested answers

Diet: Teenagers should avoid too much junk food and fizzy drinks. They should eat a healthy breakfast to help them concentrate at school/ college. They ought to eat proper meals at regular times rather than missing out meals or eating at irregular times of the day. Elderly people probably eat less as they burn up less energy, but should remember to have a balanced diet.

Sleep: Teenagers need 8–10 hours' sleep a night to function properly at school. They should be encouraged to go to bed at a reasonable time and to keep to a regular routine. Elderly people generally need less sleep but may have difficulty sleeping as they get older.

Physical exercise: This is important for any age. For teenagers physical exercise is a good way of burning excess energy and can be a sociable activity too. Elderly people should do gentle exercise such as walking, swimming, t'ai chi or yoga.

Reading p58

2 Students can either read the whole text or speed read as far as l. 37 to see how quickly they can find the answers.

Key

Ranulph Fiennes had a heart attack while boarding a plane. Health experts suggest that even if you are incredibly physically fit, your genes and family history play an important part when it comes to diseases.

3 Encourage students to read the options for each question and underline any key words. Students could compare their suggested questions in groups.

Key

1 D   2 B   3 D   4 C   5 C   6 A

Background information

Ranulph Fiennes
Sir Ranulph Fiennes has been described as the world's greatest living explorer by the Guinness Book of Records. His expeditions around the world include the first surface journey around the world's polar axis, the furthest North unsupported journey in 1986 and the first unsupported crossing of the Antarctic.

Vocabulary p60

1 Check the meaning of any unknown words, and the pronunciation of *thigh, shoulder, thumb, wrist, palm* and *calf*.

Key

arm and hand: b, h, j, k
leg and foot: a, d, m, n, p
face and head: f, g, o
torso: c, e, i, l

2 ### Key
a break/fracture: e, h, i, j, m, p
b twist: m
c sprain: h, j, m
d dislocate: b, c, h, j, m

3 When checking the dictionary entries, make sure students pay attention to any useful collocations, e.g. *heart/lung condition* (a long term health problem), *chest infection* (caused by virus or bacteria.)

Key

a bug
b infections
c condition
d ailments

Grammar p60

1 ### Key
a 'It's likely that the new Harry Potter film will break box-office records.'
b 'You'll feel much better if you do some exercise.'
c 'You can all play in the final, but you have to attend all the practice sessions tomorrow.'
d 'You don't need to work over the weekend.'
e 'Your shoulder is responding well to treatment.'

2 Refer students to the Grammar Reference if necessary.

Key

a the tense and often words that refer to time or place
b There is no need to change the tenses if the reporting verb (*say, tell*, etc.) is in the present tense or if the original statement is still relevant.

c Modal verbs *will, can, may* and *must* change. *Would, could, might, should, ought to, used to* and *had better* don't change.

3 Make sure students pay attention to any changes in time references when reporting, e.g. *today* becomes *that day*.

Key

a One of the lifeguards warned us that the beach wasn't safe for swimming off that day.
b John suddenly realised that he had left the car keys in the café.
c My brother mentioned that he and Alice were thinking of trading in their motorbike and buying a car.
d At his interview he explained that he wanted the job so much because it would allow him to travel.
e The prime suspect admitted that he'd been lying.
f Our club's top scorer boasted that he was a million times better than anyone else in the team.
g Some of the hotel guests complained that there was never anyone at the reception desk when they/you needed them.
h The driver protested that he really hadn't caused the accident.

4 ### Key

a Reporters asked the climber how long he had been training to climb Everest.
b Fans wanted to know whether Kylie was playing at last night's concert.
c In the interview Fiona was asked if/whether she had ever worked abroad.
d Our neighbours were keen to find out when we were going on holiday.
e ✓
f The taxi driver asked if/whether I would like a hand with my luggage.
g Mum wanted to know if/whether the postman had delivered the package she'd been expecting.

5 ### Key

a begged	d warned	f ask
b advise	e proposing	g reminded
c denied		

6 Key

a My boss suggested I reconsider.
b Health experts recommend eating/that we eat five portions of fresh fruit and vegetables daily.
c The celebrity model has refused to sell her story to the press.
d Haven't your parents ever forbidden you to do something?
e Are you threatening to go to the police about this?
f Your boss shouldn't promise to do something that's impossible.
g Sergeant Smith ordered his soldiers to polish their boots every day.

7 Check that students use the correct structures.

Suggested answers

a … not to talk to strangers/to be careful with money/not to get into trouble with the police.
b … borrowing her dad's car without telling him/ that we should go on a shopping spree.
c … to improve our standard of living/that they will be better leaders than the previous government.
d … to stop my pocket money for a month.
e … that it's one of my friends' birthdays/to take my books back to the library.

8 Suggested answers

a … for smashing the classroom windows.
b … of seeing her best friend behind her back.
c … for saving so many lives.
d … insisted on driving so fast.
e … from watching too much TV is to play with them more.
f … for being so rude to the press.

9 Key

a that my friends and I should get away
b we were going
c of shoplifting
d I was planning
e they go out
f to blow up

Listening p62

1 Check that students understand the meaning of *poor* in this context. Encourage them to personalise where possible with any real examples or experiences.

2 Remind students that answers are designed not to be easily guessed from reading the questions. Encourage them to note down any key words or phrases to justify their choice of answer, e.g. 1 C: *as the day progresses your energy levels drop and drop.*

Key

1 C   2 A   3 A   4 B   5 C   6 A

Tapescript

Extract 1

A: Today we're talking about what happens when you've had a bad night's sleep and, **as the day progresses, you feel your energy levels drop and drop.** So, our health expert, Alex Jones, will be giving you some advice about sleep.

B: I'm sure many of our listeners know what sleep deprivation feels like. The right amount of sleep is absolutely vital because it helps our minds and bodies function properly. It's particularly noticeable in parents with newborn babies who struggle to get off to sleep again after being woken up.

A: But it's not just parents suffering here, is it? What about the children?

B: That's a good point. Research shows that although more than two-thirds of children read to help them relax before they go to sleep, **they also spend far too long at the computer too!**

A: So how can adults and children ensure they get the sleep they need?

B: Organise a routine, such as a set bedtime, or always having a bath before bed. This will put them in the right frame of mind for the right kind of sleep.

Extract 2

A: Do you ever go into another room to do something then forget what it was you wanted to do?

B: All the time! You need to boost your brainpower. There are lots of things you can do to improve your memory.

A: You mean there are things that help to increase the size of the brain?

B: **I'm not sure if the brain actually gets bigger, although I have a feeling it can,** but its capacity increases. If you try doing puzzles like Sudoku and crosswords, you can actually increase your mental capacity quite considerably.

A: Pretty boring, if you ask me. I can think of better things to do with my time.

B: You could always try something that stimulates muscle activity. That apparently helps to activate brain cells. You're using both your brain and your body – some people do things like learning to dance.

A: No, not for me either!

B: I wasn't suggesting you should go down that route. To be honest, **I reckon you'd be better off just trying to concentrate more and focus on the job in hand.**

Extract 3

A: I realise that thousands of people have this kind of eye surgery every year, but I'm not convinced it's the right thing for me. Just how safe is it?

B: **There's no doubt that the past ten years have seen a revolution in eye surgery** and some clinics claim success rates of around 95%, but each patient's outcome will depend on different factors.

A: Meaning?

B: The bottom line is that the worse your eyesight, the more unpredictable the outcome will be.

A: And what about the claim that you'll never have to wear glasses again?

B: **Treat it with caution.** What tends to happen is that a lot of people are delighted with the treatment initially, but there can be side effects. **And whatever happens, laser treatment can't stop the normal age-related deterioration of eyesight.**

A: And do you think it matters where you have the surgery done?

B: We could recommend a reputable clinic and an experienced surgeon, who can explain the pros and cons of the treatment before you make a decision, how about that?

Speaking p62

1 Suggested answers

a a health campaign to improve public awareness
b choosing which photos would have the most impact

2 Key

How successful might these pictures be in encouraging young people stay fit and healthy? Which picture do you think should be on the cover of the leaflet?

Tapescript

Examiner: Now, I'd like you to talk about something together for about three minutes. I'd like you to imagine that the government is producing a leaflet to help young people stay fit and healthy. Here are some pictures they are considering including in the leaflet. First talk to each other about how successful these pictures might be in encouraging young people to stay fit and healthy, then decide which one should be on the cover of the leaflet.

3 Ask students which tenses the mistakes are all related to (misuse of the present continuous and the present simple). Remind them that when talking about photos or other visuals they need to choose the correct verb tense or form for, e.g. states or actions.

Key

a I think she's just about to get on her bike. Cycling is a healthy activity.
b I'm sure the message seems clear …
c This picture might encourage students to eat healthy food. The food looks quite tempting, doesn't it?
d And here they're in a gym. This should encourage people to take more exercise.
e This picture of visiting/a visit to the dentist …
f She seems to be drinking mineral water. It's vital to drink water when you exercise.
g So do we agree that … ?

4 Set a time limit of four minutes for students to do the activity. Refer students back to the *How to do it* box on page 50 if necessary.

5 Insist on the importance of expanding on ideas for Part 4 questions. Point out that the questions/ advice in the prompt sections encourage candidates to personalise their answers or to develop an argument by considering alternative points of view. Remind them that they don't have to agree with each other when answering the questions.

There is authentic practice of this section on page 96 of the Workbook.

Use of English p64

1 Before reading, ask students if they can identify the insect in the photo. Check the spelling (*mosquito*) and ask what disease it can spread (*malaria*).

Key

1 c

2 After students have read the *tip* box and completed the gaps, ask them to check in a dictionary to see if they can find the correct part of speech by looking under each head word in the task, e.g. misery (n) > miserable (adj).

Key

1 miserable	6 environmental
2 hazardous	7 intervention
3 carriers	8 expertly
4 scientists	9 incurable
5 mismanagement	10 treatment

Remind students to check for any possible spelling errors once they have completed both texts.

Vocabulary p65

1 Remind students to look carefully at what part of speech is missing.

Key

a perfectionist	c provision
b believer	d attendance

2 Encourage students to use a dictionary to complete the task.

Key

	verb	noun (thing)	noun (person)	adjective	adverb
a	produce	product productivity	producer	produced productive	productively
b	perfect	perfection	perfectionist	perfect	perfectly
c	authorise	authority authorisation	authority	authoritarian authoritative	authoritatively
d	_____	medicine	medic	medicinal medical	medicinally medically
e	provide	provision	provider	—————	
f	manage	management	manager	managed manageable	manageably
g	believe	belief	believer	believed believable	believably
h	—————	expertise	expert	expert	expertly
i	—————	fortune		fortunate	fortunately
j	attend	attendance attention	attendant attender	—————	—————

Optional activity

In pairs, students write three or four sentences that have a space for some of the words from the table. Students pass their sentences to another pair who try to complete the sentences with the correct part of speech.

3 Remind students to check the pronunciation and word stress when using the dictionary, e.g. /ˈperfect/ (adjective) but /perˈfect/ (verb).

Key

produce	product	producer
productive	productively	

perfect	perfection	perfectionist
perfect	perfectly	

Optional activity

Encourage students to use dictionaries to check or find the correct forms. Students might like to write one or two questions to ask and answer in pairs or groups, e.g. *How tolerant do you think you are? What's the most unforgettable experience you've had this year?*

4 Make sure students check spelling of individual words.

Key

a	forgettable	e	desirable
b	avoidable	f	predictable
c	tolerable	g	agreeable
d	acceptable	h	explicable

5 Give an example yourself to help students if necessary. Encourage them to ask follow up questions where possible.

Key

a	unforgettable	e	undesirable
b	unavoidable	f	unpredictable
c	intolerable	g	disagreeable
d	unacceptable	h	inexplicable

Writing p66

1 Ask students if any of them have ever visited a spa or health centre and whether they enjoyed it. Remind them to underline key words in the exam task in order to focus on the information necessary to complete the task.

Key

a You must write a letter to the manager of the spa.
b You should comment on the negative and positive aspects.
c You should say how improvements could be made to the spa for future visits.

2 Once students have decided on suitable answers refer them to the Writing Guide to remind themselves of the basic layout and structure of formal letters.

Key

1 b   2 c   3 b   4 c

3 Point out to students that by making their own notes in this way, then expanding on them (as they will do in 4 and 5), it will help them avoid copying extracts direct from the input text.

Key

positive: helpful range of talks
negative points: not enough different sizes in shop, most groups full

4 Suggested answers

not enough different sizes in shop – stock a wider range of sizes
groups full – limit number of people per group

5 Encourage students to try to use their own words and not simply copy from the brochure. Make sure they are using an appropriate formal style where possible.

Suggested answers

I would suggest that you stock a wider range of clothes sizes in the shop as there was a very limited choice. There was an excellent selection of talks which were very informative.
Although a wide range of sports activities are offered, most of the groups were full. It might be a good idea to limit the number of people per group.

6 Key

a use name – Dear Mr Newton
c too informal – Although we wish to refer to these negative aspects, there were also several very positive ones.
e too informal – We consider the price of clothes and equipment in the shop to be exhorbitant.
f too informal – We would suggest you devise a better booking system.

For an assessed authentic answer to this Writing task, see page 5 of the *Writing and Speaking Assessment Booklet* in the Teacher's Pack.

Review p68

1 Key
a 8   b 6   c 2   d 1   e 7   f 4   g 3   h 5

2 Key

a	on	e	under
b	running	f	dislocated
c	ache	g	pull
d	broken/fractured	h	sprained

3 Key

a	prevention (8)	e	manageable (3)
b	Intervention (6)	f	survivors (1)
c	technically (5)	g	predictions (4)
d	threatening (7)	h	mechanical (2)

4 Key

1	memorable	5	inexplicable
2	predictable	6	avoidable
3	agreeable	7	unacceptable
4	acceptable	8	desirable

Would you believe it?

Lead in p69

1 Before students discuss the statements, go over some useful language that will help them structure their ideas and expand any reasons they give, e.g. modal verbs *must/might/can't be true/false*. The Grammar section in this unit relates to modals. Check students know what *celery* is.

2 Check the meaning of any difficult vocabulary. e.g. *something fishy* (d), *sued* (e).

Key

a	true	d	true	g	true
b	false	e	true	h	false
c	false	f	false		

Ask students to reword the phrases or sentences to show they have understood the meaning.

Suggested answers

a come true – become reality
b give a false impression – (usually) make something appear better than it really is
c under false pretences – by lying
d doesn't ring true – doesn't sound/appear true
e not strictly true – not completely accurate
f a false economy – something that seems to save you money but doesn't in the long run
g a dream come true – something you've always wished for
h a false sense of security – something that makes you feel safe but cannot be relied on

Reading p70

1 Ask if any students are fans of these comic book heroes and who has seen any of the Spider-man, Superman or Hulk films and what they think of them. Ask them to name any women superheroes, e.g. Wonderwoman, Elektra.

Key

1C Daredevil has radar sense.
2A Spider-man can stick to surfaces like a spider and can climb buildings with his bare hands.
3B Superman can fly at high speed, has superhuman strength, can jump up/over buildings and has X-ray vision.
4E The Incredible Hulk has superhuman strength.
5D Magneto can create electromagnetic fields and levitate objects made of metal, project forcefields and generate electricity.

2 Encourage students to try and find the answers without dictionaries before checking any vocabulary they might have difficulties with. Make sure they look for synonyms or similar words/expressions for the underlined words in 1–12.

Key

1 B 2 A 3 C 4 B/D 5 B/D 6 A 7 C/E
8 C/E 9 B 10 E 11 D 12 E

1 substance – *a chemical called chlorophyll* (l. 33), speeds up – *accelerates* (l. 34)
2 substance – *silk* (l. 15), looks weaker – *deceptively strong, despite its gossamer appearance* (l. 15)
3 system – *radar sense* (l. 45), limited vision – *blinding him permanently* (l. 43)
4/5 someone … away from his home – *forced to flee his doomed planet* (l. 21)/*isolated himself from humanity* (l. 66)
6 substance – *sticky silk* (l. 10), creatures – *spiders* (l. 9), secure themselves – *anchors them in position* (l. 11)
7/8 selfless act – *saved a man from being hit by a truck* (l. 42)/*Banner saved him* (l. 89)
9 new identity – *adopted under the name Clark Kent* (l. 22), young age – *As a child* (l. 21)
10 creature – *the cuttlefish* (l. 107), changing the way it looks – *alter their appearance* (l. 107)
11 form of transport – *trains that float over the rails* (l.-76)
12 substances – *natural chemicals* (l. 101), discomfort less noticeable – *mask the pain* (l. 101)

Vocabulary p72

1 Refer students back to the Reading text on page 70 to find the verb *creep* (l. 2). Ask them to work out the meaning from context and decide if it is a verb of moving or looking. Encourage use of dictionaries for checking answers.

Key

a glance   d glare
b gaze   e peep
c glimpse
They are all verbs of looking.

2 Make sure students pay attention to any changes in form they need to make.

Key

a crawl   d tripping/limping
b plod   e tripping/stumbling
c creeped

3 Key

a glance
b gaze
c glimpse
d glare

Grammar p72

1 Before doing the exercise tell students to quickly find examples of modal verbs used in the Reading text on pages 70–71 (*can, could, have to, would, may*).

Key

a could 6   d can 3   f don't need to 2
b must 1   e should 7   g must 4
c might 5

2 Students work in pairs or small groups then compare their answers with other students.

Key

a True. It's been opened.
b False. They broke in through the window.
c True. We don't know who called the police but they are there now.
d True. It's unclear how many sets of footprints there are.
e False. The safe doesn't appear to have any valuables in.
f True. A policeman is looking at something through his magnifying glass.
g False. It's unlikely there was anyone at home.

3 Key

1 must have stolen   4 can't have done
2 might have come   5 should have been
3 might have left   6 might have handed

4 Remind students that we use *be able to* in the past for achievements and not *could*.

Key

a couldn't
b might/may/will be able to
c was able to
d couldn't/haven't been able to
e can't
f was able to
g being able to

5 Key

a needn't have bothered
b don't need to worry
c didn't need to pay
d don't need to do/needn't do
e needn't apply/don't need to
f needn't have packed

6 Key

a can't be   d were able to
b don't have to   e might not be
c must be

7 You might like to give an example of a game/sport first to see if students can guess it.

Key

a 3   b 5   c 2   d 4   e 1

Listening p74

1 Check students understand the difference between *alive* (not dead) and *live* (not recorded). Ask students about their experiences of live concerts and whether they prefer to listen to music at home and why. You could develop the discussion into different ways of listening to music and some of the issues involved (cost of CDs, downloading music from the Internet, quality, cost, piracy, etc.).

2 Encourage students to make notes of any key words/phrases while listening to support their answers.

Key

a He was impressed by their charisma and good looks.

b They became an overnight music success and won a major music award.

c They had no musical talent and mimed or 'lip-synched'.

d While they were performing 'live' on MTV the record jumped.

e The music world was shocked and they had to give back an award.

Tapescript

Some years ago, record producer Frank Farian discovered Robert Pilatus and Fabrice Morvan, otherwise known as Rob and Fab, in Munich. **Impressed by their charisma and chiselled good looks,** Farian formed them into pop group *Milli Vanilli*. Their success was almost instantaneous. **They rocketed to stardom on the strength of two hit singles. Their debut album sold over seven million copies, and they won a major music award as best new artist.** But there was an ugly truth lurking behind the attractive façade presented by the duo. **They possessed no musical abilities whatsoever.** They couldn't play instruments, write music, or even sing. All of their songs had been created in a studio by professional musicians. Whenever they performed on stage, they simply mimed, or 'lip-synched' the words. Embarrassed by the situation, Rob and Fab confronted Farian and insisted that he allow them to sing on their next album. However, following **a supposedly live performance on MTV, when the record they were miming to 'jumped',** Farian revealed that their act was a sham. **The news rocked the music industry** – the media latched onto the story with a passion and **they were stripped of their award.** For many, Rob and Fab's deception was a perfect representation of the artificial, pre-packaged nature of the pop music industry itself.

3 Key

1 H   2 G   3 D   4 E   5 B   6 F   7 H   8 B
9 D   10 A

Tapescript

Speaker 1
Well, some pop groups do lip-synch, and manage not to look awkward, but it's a dangerous game. One singer famously mimed out of synch because she couldn't hear her band's live backing track! But whether this should happen is debatable. If you purchase very expensive tickets for a live performance, you expect just that – otherwise it's a fraud. You might as well just listen to the CD at home instead of travelling to the show. **If they say on their advertising that it's mimed, then that's fair enough** – we can make our choice based on information. **Mostly it's about poor singers who can't perform live,** and that's the difference between studio singers and great and long-lasting talent.

Speaker 2
I appreciate the fact that artists like Britney Spears have active dance routines to perform and therefore think this justifies them miming. But if you went to a musical and the performers simply mimed to a backing track, you'd demand your money back! **Considering the expense and difficulty of getting tickets to these concerts** – not to mention the expectation that you're going to see your favourite artist sing live – that's what you should get! **I think it is absolutely outrageous when so-called 'pop stars' mime in front of hundreds of fans.** You can pay a fortune to see such artists perform – the least they can do is sing live.

Speaker 3
Singers who can't sing live highlight all that's wrong with the music industry. **It's an industry full of manufactured bands and artists whose records are sold purely on their appearance** – not their musical ability. I have a lot of respect for artists like Beyonce, who are amazing live and obviously very talented. **In my opinion, if you can't perform live, you aren't a musician.** I feel very dejected that the music industry is no longer about talent. It is all about: if your face fits, your voice can always be altered to make it sound good. You never hear of opera singers miming, so why should pop stars be able to get away with it?

Speaker 4
Last week I went to see a group of amateurs performing a musical. **The performers all had small mikes taped to them, and they sang and danced fantastically well at the same time. You'd never have guessed these people were amateurs,** and were fitting all this in with their day jobs. If they can perform so expertly for free, then pop stars should be able to do it for the thousands they're paid. **And**

if artists can't perform live on TV, they should show a video instead. If performers can't do everything live, they should work on their act more until they can. Anyone who's a singer–dancer should able to do both without miming. If they can't, they're cheating the audience.

Speaker 5
Music hasn't really been 'live' for years. It's usually from a backing track and often performed by computer, so why should anyone expect singing to be live as well? **When you buy pop music, you aren't buying music, but an eye-catching, shiny, plastic package conforming to the styles and stereotypes of the day.** The press really needs to give up this lip-synching coverage. **If artists who do amazing dance routines sang live, they would sound winded and out of tune.** It would be impossible to dance like they do and sing so that it sounds as good as their recordings. The fact that some lip-synching may take place never enters my mind.

4 Ask students if they agreed with the views of any of the speakers. Ask if they can name any artists who never lip-synch.

Speaking p75

1 Ask students to look quickly at the photos and see if they can establish a common theme, e.g. dressing up/costumes.

Key
1 Rupert the Bear (fictional children's character)
2 fancy dress
3 Japanese make up
4 Indian boy

2 Key
a 1/2/4 b 4 c 4 d 1/2/4 e 1/2/4

3 Encourage students to give reasons and hypothesise with their suggested answers.

Suggested answers
excited at the thought of something: 1, 2, 3
lost in a world of their own: 3, 4
committed to what they are doing: 2, 3
apprehensive about what might happen: 4
self-conscious about their appearance: 1, 2

4 Remind students that they shouldn't simply describe the photos but to try and compare or make links between them. Encourage them to try to use some of the language from exercises 2 and 3.

5 Candidates only have a very short time to answer the follow-up question so they should try to be succinct. Check students understand *I'm torn between* in the *Making decisions and giving reasons* phrases.

There is an authentic practice of this section on page 96 of the Workbook.

Use of English p76

1 Ask students if they play tricks on April 1st (or an equivalent day). If so, ask whether their newspapers, radio stations or TV channels join in and if they can think of any good examples of tricks.

2 Key
A fast food chain pretended that they had invented a left-handed burger to fool customers.

3 Remind students to look carefully at the parts of speech before and after each gap and to pay attention to prepositions which may collocate with specific words, e.g. according to. Students could check in a dictionary after completing the task.

Key

1	A	5	D	9	A
2	D	6	A	10	B
3	A	7	B	11	C
4	B	8	B	12	D

For extra practice with dictionaries and Use of English, Part 1 see Worksheet 7 in the *Using a dictionary for exams* booklet in the Teacher's Pack.

4 Encourage students to use a dictionary if they are not sure of the meaning.

Key

a 3   b 4   c 2   d 1

5 Remind students not to change the key word and to look carefully at tenses and form.

Key

a who came up with
b can I get hold of
c is no point in working
d was taken in by

Vocabulary p77

1 If students have access to dictionaries encourage them to look up or check the meaning of expressions they don't know or can't guess.

Key

a I completely agree
b return soon
c according to what is proper
d everywhere
e immediately
f get him to like you
g had justice on his side

2 Key
a 3   b 2   c 1   d 4

Writing p78

1 Ask students to refer to the photos and say what possible effects computers and games might have on people.

2 Suggested answers

+

They develop interactive skills and test intelligence.
They can be educational, e.g. games which teach children to take care of animals, etc.

−

They stop people from doing other activities such as reading, sports, etc.
A lot of parents don't have enough control or check the content of children's games.

3 Students should be aware of the criteria used for marking Paper 2. These can be found in the Cambridge ESOL CAE Handbook. Encourage them to come up with practical suggestions for getting good marks, where possible.

Key and suggested answers

a 5 Check for basic errors like missing capital letters, subject–verb agreement, verbs in the right tense, etc.
b 3 Check for appropriacy of linking words according to whether the register is more formal or informal. Make sure sentences aren't too staccato and short. Try to vary how sentences are structured and linked.
c 6 Include language relevant to the task, e.g. if you're writing an article for a magazine you would probably need to include language of description, evaluation and opinion, as well as relevant vocabulary for the topic. Try to refer to the same things in different ways by using a different word or rephrasing so as to avoid repetition.
d 2 Make a clear plan before you start writing and organise relevant ideas under paragraph headings. Students should be aware of the different formats required for different task types (see the Writing Guide).
e 1 Make sure you read the question and any input information carefully. Students should be encouraged to underline key words.
f 4 Think about the purpose of the writing task and who it is for in order to decide on the appropriate register.

4 Key
a The introduction is good, with interesting questions for the reader. There are some good for and against arguments in the paragraphs, but the ideas are not well linked and the essay all seems rather disjointed.

b Generally, yes.

c The arguments for and against are divided clearly although there are no defined topic sentences.

d No. More use of linkers needed, especially in paragraph 2. The sentences are short and disconnected. The words and phrases used seem appropriate.

e There is a good use of modal verbs throughout for speculation and some good use of words and expressions, e.g. distinguish what is reality from fantasy, desensitised to suffering, addictive nature of games, let off steam, etc.

f No

5 Key

a 8, 10
b 1, 5, 7, 8, 9, 10
c 2, 3, 4, 6

6 Monitor students and make sure they are aware of any structural changes needed to the sentences. Encourage them to use link words from exercise 5, but they may use other ideas of their own.

Suggested answers

a Computer games are good fun. What is more/Furthermore, they can be very social.

b One concern is that young people may have trouble distinguishing what is real from what is fantasy. As a consequence/result/Therefore, they may act out what they do in games in real life.
Or ... fantasy, which is why they may act out ...

c There is a great deal of violence in fairy tales. However, it never lead our parents or grandparents to behave violently in real life.

d A lot of violent computer games are interactive. As a consequence/result/Therefore/What is more, they may be more harmful than violent films on television.
Or ... interactive which is why they may be more harmful ...

e Children might identify with the aggressive characters on screen. As a consequence/result/Therefore/Furthermore, they might try to solve their problems in a violent way too.
Or ... on screen which is why they might try to solve ...

f The games sometimes take over children's lives. Therefore/As a consequence/result, children often suffer psychologically.
Or ... children's lives which is why/so that children often suffer ...

g Ultra-violent video games are unhealthy. However, there is no proof that they turn normal children into killers.
Or
Despite/In spite of ultra-violent video games being unhealthy, there is no proof that they turn normal children into killers.

For an assessed authentic answer to this writing task, see page 11 of the *Writing and Speaking Assessment Booklet* in the Teacher's Pack.

Review p80

1 Key

a didn't ring true
b under false pretences
c false economy to buy

2 Key

a plod   c stumble
b stagger   d gaze

3 Key

a glance   c crawl   e creep
b leap   d march

4 Key

a about   b to   c in   d about   e at

5 Key

1 right away/now   4 left feet
2 left ... right   5 leftovers
3 the right   6 By rights

6 Key

1 Despite   5 so that
2 as well as   6 although/while
3 On the other hand   7 while/although
4 After

Traces of the past

Lead in p81

1 a, b

Once students have identified the different periods of history shown, ask which they would have liked to live in (or not) and why.

Key

1 Ancient Rome (from 753 BC to 476 AD) or Greece (from roughly 1700 to 146 BC)
2 Ancient Egypt (roughly 3100 BC to 395 AD)
3 the Renaissance (fifteenth to sixteenth century; the illustration is a da Vinci sketch)
4 the 1960s (the photo is from the Vietnam War)
5 Middle Ages or Medieval times (between the end of the Roman Empire and the Renaissance)
6 prehistory

1 c

Ask students to think about how reliable different sources of information might be, e.g. depending on the author, history books may be written with a certain bias.

Suggested answers

Information may come from various sources depending on the period. For more modern times we have written or photographic documentation or film footage, and for older times historians rely on archaeological evidence.

1 d

Encourage students to think beyond the immediate effects of each period and consider whether we are still influenced today by any of these periods and their events.

Suggested answers

Ancient Greece and Rome were the source of many ideas that people believe in today, such as democracy as well as art and drama, Mathematics and civil engineering.
The Ancient Egyptians had an advanced understanding of science, medicine, astronomy and architecture, as well as excellent craftsmanship.

The Renaissance resulted in new movements in art, music and literature.
The 1960s and the Vietnam War were directly responsible for social unrest and peace movements in the United States. The 1960s also saw important developments in music, art and literature and the role of young people in society.
In the Middle Ages much of the knowledge and expertise from previous periods was lost during years of war, religious crusades and civil unrest.
Prehistory laid the foundations of civilisation in terms of social organisation, farming and developments in craftsmanship.

Reading p82

1 Ask students to look at the photos and titles or the first few lines of each extract to see if they can match them up quickly.

Key

a Extract from a novel
b Genealogy
c Wanted Roman Soldiers!

2 Refer students to the *tip* box. Remind them to read the questions carefully before reading the extracts. Encourage them to underline or note where they found the evidence to justify their answers.

Key

1 C 2 A 3 A 4 C 5 B 6 C

Optional activity

Students divide into pairs and choose two or three new words or expressions from one extract per pair. Ask students to check meanings in a dictionary, and then pairs can teach other pairs their words/expressions from individual extracts.

Vocabulary p84

1 If students find this difficult, you may want to refer them to exercise 2 first and ask them to complete each space with a suitable meaning from a–h. Encourage use of dictionaries for checking answers.

Key

1 a set b setting
2 a gave b give
3 a put b put
4 a take b taken

2 Key

a 1b b 4b c 3a d 4a e 1a f 3b g 2b h 2a

3 Students should note that dictionaries entries normally show definitions in order of frequency of use, so students need to scan the complete entry. Encourage students to look at example sentences in the dictionary with the phrasal verbs in context.

Key

Suggested answers

a snow/bad weather
b gases/fumes
c (s)he cut my hair really short
d to buy them a present

Grammar p84

1 Point out that participle clauses usually make a sentence sound more formal and are used in written rather than spoken statements. Refer students to the Grammar Reference for further information about participle clauses as they work through the exercises in this section.

Key

a 4 b 3 c 6 d 2 e 5 f 1

Optional activity

Ask students to rewrite the sentences in a–f to illustrate their function. There may be more than one answer.

a If plants are grown in the right conditions, they will flower all summer.
b After he had parked his car in a side road, he strolled towards the town centre.
c A massive earthquake has hit parts of India and left thousands of people homeless.
d A group of archaeologists who are exploring the island have discovered the skeleton of a new species of human being.
e Because we didn't have a mobile phone, we were unable to ring our hosts …
f After he had finished his medical training, my brother decided …

2 Compare answers as a class, as students may suggest different answers. Make sure that they make any other necessary changes to incorporate the participle clause.

Suggested answers

a Stolen from the Munch Museum, *The Scream* is worth millions of pounds.
Worth millions of pounds, *The Scream* was stolen from the Munch Museum.
b Washed with care, woollen sweaters will retain their shape.
c Hoping to confirm the suspect's part in the robbery, the detectives arranged an identity parade.
d Crossing the finishing line, the winner raises his hands in triumph!
e Having undergone final medical checks, the explorer will set out on his polar expedition.
f Not realising how dangerous the snake was, the toddler reached out towards it.

3 Remind students of the importance of correct spelling.

Key

a	making	d	offering	g	travelling
b	building	e	preferring	h	arguing
c	stopping	f	lying	i	occurring

4 Remind students of the importance of correct spelling.

Key

a	bitten	f	flew	k	sold
b	brought	g	hidden	l	set
c	caught	h	left	m	spoken
d	driven	i	met	n	woken
e	fought	j	proven/proved		

5 Check students are clear which verb in each sentence should change to the participle form, before they rewrite the sentences. Elicit that in b) and e), depending on the context, it doesn't matter which of the verbs becomes the participle, but elicit why there is no choice with the others (they wouldn't make sense).

Key

a   After spending 10 hours trapped underground, a group of cavers has/have finally been rescued.

b   While admitting that driving at excessive speeds is dangerous, I don't accept we should have speed cameras everywhere.
While not accepting that we should have speed cameras everywhere, I admit that driving at excessive speeds is dangerous.

c   Not being a local, he didn't know the area.

d   On hearing that a peace treaty had been signed, civilians began celebrating in the streets.

e   Although sympathising with her situation, the judge didn't agree with the defendant's actions.
Although not agreeing with the defendant's actions, the judge did sympathise with her situation.

6 Suggested answers

a   The girl fled from the lion while/as it roared ferociously. (Without rewording, it means the girl is roaring ferociously, not the lion.)

b   Two of the terrorists that/who shot the President have been caught. (The participle cannot be used to refer to something that happened in the past.)

c   The man who invented the digital camera has won an award. (As sentence b)

d   Because no one wanted to spoil the fun, the wedding celebrations went on well into the night. (As sentence a, the participle has to refer to the subject of the next clause, *the wedding celebrations*, which would not make sense.)

e   If things are planted with care, novice gardeners will be amazed how easy it is to grow them. (As with sentences a and d, without rewording the participle refers to the gardeners.)

f   Having passed his driving test, Gary became rather big-headed. (As sentence b)

7 Point out that students should not overuse participle forms in their own writing. Check any unknown vocabulary.

Key

1   Having spent three days …

2   Wanting to become …

3   Having no way/Not having any way of transporting possesions, he took …

4   Having made good progress at first, he then experienced …

5   meaning that the temperature …

6   preventing him from...

7   Feeling desperate, Ben searched …

8   Having no/Not having any advanced technical equipement …

9   Taking out his shovel he dug …

10   saving Ben …

Listening p86

1 Remind students that, in Part 2, reading the questions first and speculating on the content can be a useful way of focusing on the task. They should also be prepared to listen out for synonymous language that will cue the answer to a question.

Check students understand the meaning of *shipwreck*.

Suggested answers

1 popular, because of
2 find
3 set off, set out from
4 find shelter/a safe place
5 before them/ahead of them
6 broken
7 Even though, sailors on deck/crew
8 acceptable/right

2 Refer students to the *tip* box before listening.

Key

1	seabed/sea bed	5	entrance
2	gold coins	6	bridge
3	1807	7	safety
4	gale	8	sea conditions

Tapescript

As you all know, The Lizard is a very popular area for divers, both amateur and professional, and this is because of **the number of accessible wrecks that litter the seabed.** Today I'd like to tell you why there are so many in this area. The Lizard is the biggest trap for shipping in British waters. It juts out into the Channel to welcome sailors home to England … and to sink them by the thousand on its reefs and cliffs. In fact, because of the hazards posed by the Lizard's cliffs and underwater reefs the Admiralty advises navigators to keep three or more miles off shore in bad weather. And those that didn't listen, well, they've made the Lizard a good diving ground!

The wrecks of The Lizard date back centuries and many contain real treasure – and I mean real treasure. For example, **divers can easily find gold coins.** A lot have already been recovered but I'm sure there are still more down there. The diving is especially good on the reefs offshore from Porthleven to Lizard Point. This is basically one big sailing-ship graveyard – there are cannons on almost every 500m of seabed!

On 24 December 1807, the HMS Anson set off from Falmouth and was sadly destined to become one of these wrecks. She was setting sail to join patrols trying to block the French ports, but by the time Captain Charles Lydiard reached the French coast, **she was running into a severe gale and finally had to turn homewards to seek shelter** in Falmouth again.

The Anson was in real trouble and the crew must have been overjoyed to see the safety of land. But imagine how they felt when **they realised it was not the entrance back into Falmouth** but the dreaded Lizard. Lydiard tried to sail her out of the trap but by then she was dipping her head into the huge seas and, slowly but surely, she was being blown into danger. She hit an uncharted reef of rock just 100 metres from the beach. The ship shuddered and her main mast broke. In the enormous seas there was little chance of survival for the crew. **The mast, however, had fallen onto the beach and formed a sort of bridge** which some sailors were lucky enough to use. Captain Lydiard was not one of the lucky ones. He died in the surf on the beach – as did 190 out of the 330 men aboard. Even though people on the beach tried desperately to help the men, the waves were just too strong and **they died only feet from safety.** And the Anson joined countless other wrecks.

Cannons from the Anson are still there today – just 100 metres off the beach, and gold coins can occasionally be found. Diving the Anson is fascinating, I'd really recommend it, but … **you must make sure the sea conditions are right.** Diving here can be very dangerous indeed.

Speaking p86

1 Put students into pairs or small groups and see who can think of the best heading for the group of photos, e.g. *Aspects of the past/Learning about the past*. Remind them of the exercises on page 81 if they need some ideas. Encourage them to brainstorm vocabulary relevant to each photo before they look at exercise 2, and then compare their ideas with the words and phrases suggested.

Suggested answer

They may be asked to talk about different ways we can find out about the past and what the advantages and disadvantages of each one are, which is more accurate, or which is more rewarding.

2 Check the meaning of any unknown words, e.g. *dig, excavation, footage, manuscripts,* and *re-enactment.*

Key

a 4   b 3   c 2   d 5   e 3, 6   f 2   g 1   h 6   i 5

3 Monitor pairs of students and make sure they are keeping to the time limit. Check they are answering both parts of the question and not just describing the photos.

4 Set a time limit of 30 seconds for this follow-up question and encourage students to justify their answers.

Suggested answers

More accurate information may come from film footage or documentary evidence. There could be an element of speculation about the archaeological dig, and some element of entertainment to the battle re-enactment and traditional craftsmen. The personal documents have the advantage that they are written by 'real' people at the time, but may also be emotionally or personally biased and not as objectively factual.

There is authentic practice of this section on page 96 of the Workbook.

Use of English p88

1 If you have younger students, find out what periods of history they are studying and what methods they use to learn about it apart from books. Older students may have more perspective on how understanding history helps to give a fuller understanding of many other subjects, and that we can learn from history not to repeat mistakes.

2 Key
Herodotus (c.484–425 BC) was the first person to study, and report on, events in different countries from his own.

3 Refer students to the *tip* box. Remind them to look carefully at which part of speech might fit in the gaps and to pay attention to context e.g. 3 *skilful* links to the positive adjectives *informative* and *lively.* Encourage students to check in a dictionary for possible correct answers and spelling.

Key

1	passionate	4	unforgettable
2	extensively	5	perception
3	skilful		

4 Key

6	dramatically	9	development
7	archaeologists	10	civilisations
8	enabled		

Optional activity

Before checking the answers with the whole class, ask students to check the pronunciation and word stress of the missing words in a dictionary.

Vocabulary p89

1 Encourage students to use dictionaries for tasks 1 and 2. Make sure they pay attention to word stress and pronunciation, e.g. de<u>mo</u>cracy, demo<u>cra</u>tic.

Key

a	evidence	e	awareness
b	adaptability	f	accuracy
c	significance	g	democracy
d	ambition	h	independence

2 Key

a	impractical	g	immoral
b	indecisive	h	irregular
c	incapable	i	illegal
d	irrelevant	j	disagreeable
e	unsuitable	k	dishonest
f	illogical		

3 Key
im before the letters *p* and *m.*
il before the letter *l.*
ir before the letter *r.*

4 Set a time limit and see how many examples students can find in pairs or small groups, e.g. *unlimited, unlucky, unmistakable, unmanageable, unpleasant, unpopular, unreliable, unrealistic*.

> **Optional activity**
>
> Students choose two or three of the adjectives with the suffix *un* they found in the dictionary and write a gapped sentence for each one with the adjective missing. Students pass on their sentences and test each other.

5 Ask students to suggest examples of words for each prefix, e.g. *cooperation*.

Key

a	trans	d	mis	f	over
b	un	e	inter	g	under
c	co				

6 **Key**

a	transatlantic	d	interdepartmental
b	undercooked	e	unlock
c	misunderstood	f	coexisted

Writing p90

1 You might like to divide students up into pairs/small groups and ask them to think about one of the areas before regrouping them to share ideas. Encourage them to give reasons for their answers. The photos in this section might give them some ideas.

2 Students will probably be able to identify the events quickly by looking at the photos. Ask one or two follow-up questions, e.g.

Why was Neil Armstrong's achievement so great? How did people celebrate the fall of the Berlin Wall? What potential problems did the birth of Dolly create?

Ask students what important twentieth century events the other photos depict. You might want to expand by asking what they think has been the most significant event so far of the twenty-first century.

Key

A the first man on the moon
B the fall of the Berlin Wall
C the first animal to be cloned

3 Suggest students underline the verb tenses in each paragraph to focus on the different uses.

Key

a C, A, B
b first: A, middle: B, last: C
c Paragraph A and B: narrative tenses, past simple/continuous and past perfect
Paragraph C: there are more present tenses and modal verbs for hypothesis.

4 You might like to set this exercise for homework and ask students to discuss and share information about the events in the next class. Remind them of the Reading text about holidays in space (page 35) when discussing A.

Suggested answers

A Neil Armstrong was the first man to land on the moon in 1969. He was joined by colleague Buzz Aldrin. This was the culmination of the space race between the United States and the Soviet Union. In 2001 the first space tourist went into space, and the Cassini spacecraft has sent back images of Saturn. Scientists are investigating the possibilities of terraforming other planets so that they could support human life.

B The Berlin Wall fell in November 1989 allowing people from Communist East Berlin to flood into West Berlin. At the end of the Second World War, Germany was divided between the Allies, and East Berlin fell under Communist rule. The Wall was built in 1961 to stop people moving from East to West Berlin. The fall of the Wall became a symbol of the collapse of Communism in Eastern Europe and the end of the Cold War.

C Dolly was cloned in 1996 in the UK. Directly involved were the scientists responsible. The breakthrough led to great public and scientific debate about the ethics of cloning, as opposed to 'natural' reproduction. The science that produced Dolly wasn't new, and technically she wasn't the first clone, but was the most famous example of it. There are many potential developments for farming as well as potential breakthroughs in human medicine.

5 Encourage students to research information about a significant event before they try and answer the question, in order to structure their ideas for the task in 8. Remind them of the importance of making a plan for Paper 2 to ensure they have enough information to answer all parts of the question before starting to write.

6 Ask students if they can think of a noun to collocate with each of the adjectives, or a recent news story they could apply these adjectives to.

Key

a	neutral	e	positive	h	neutral
b	positive	f	neutral	i	negative
c	neutral	g	negative	j	negative
d	negative				

7 Suggested answers
   a devastating/catastrophic
   b significant/inspirational/momentous
   c significant/beneficial/momentous
   d significant/devastating/momentous/ catastrophic/grave
   e significant/devastating/momentous/ unforeseen/grave

For an assessed authentic answer to this Writing task, see page 12 of the *Writing and Speaking Assessment Booklet* in the Teacher's Pack.

Review p92

1 Key
a in   b of   c to   d in   e for

2 Key

a	taking	d	set	g	set
b	turned	e	turn	h	put
c	giving	f	put		

3 Key
   b 5 significant
   c 1 comparative
   d 3 extensive
   e 6 perceptive
   f 2 dramatic

4 Key

a	irrelevant	e	incapable
b	illegal	f	indecisive
c	dishonest	g	unsuitable
d	immoral	h	illogical

5 Key

a	evidence	d	awareness
b	accuracy	e	independence
c	Ambition		

6 Key

a	unfasten	e	misinformed
b	cooperate	f	international
c	transcontinental	g	underestimated
d	overcooked		

7 Key

1	inspirational	4	significant
2	devastating	5	beneficial
3	catastrophic	6	unforeseen

The big issues

Lead in p93

1 Make sure students understand the expression *burning issues* (most important/crucial ones). If students discuss this in small groups, ask each group to explain which area they ranked first, giving reasons why.

2 Key

A aid
B education
C technology

3 Point out that the speakers make reference to all three statements in each extract but students should listen for the overall view given by each speaker.

Key

A 3
B 1
C 1

Tapescript

Speaker 1

The trouble is that it's not simply a question of handing out vast sums of money. The whole concept of aid is an extremely complex one. It's different, of course, if there's been some kind of natural disaster, like a flood or drought. Aid has to be something tangible in cases like these, and it has to arrive quickly. But in the long-term, giving money is not necessarily a good idea, so we have to work out how we can best help people in need. Some of the best aid programmes are those which concentrate on showing people how they can better their own situation themselves, for example, by showing them new farming techniques, or setting up small businesses which provide work for the local population. These schemes often produce extremely beneficial results which last.

Speaker 2

With hindsight, people come out with statements like 'School days are the best days of your life', and so on. But at the time it often doesn't seem like that. Many young people can't wait to leave school and start earning a living. So in a way, we have to educate them to understand the value of education, if you see what I mean. Perhaps the mistake we've made is to set up an educational system which is too academic. Maybe it should be more practically orientated. But the problem with that is that it pushes you in a certain direction at a very early age – and then you're locked into a career path you might regret later on.

Speaker 3

I once saw a film about a machine capable of controlling the whole human race. At the time we all thought this was pure fantasy – but I'm not so sure now. We know that the power of the human brain will always exceed that of any machine, simply because it has logic. But we tend to rely more and more on technology to do what for us would be extremely time-consuming activities. I sometimes wonder if our brains will simply stop working because they haven't got enough to occupy them! I know it seems a bit far-fetched but maybe it could happen!

4 Where possible, ask students to brainstorm for and against the statements before they give their opinions. See if they can remember any of the reasons/opinions given by the speakers in exercise 3 to support their arguments.

Reading p94

1 Suggested answers

Films: *Robots, I, Robot, Toy Story, The Matrix, AI, The Terminator, Blade Runner, Robocop, Star Trek, Star Wars, 2001: A Space Odyssey.*
Books: *The Hitchhiker's Guide to the Galaxy*

2 Ask students to match the meanings before looking at the text. Later, they can check the answers in context after they have completed exercise 3.

Key

a (l. 4) 2		d (l. 37) 5	
b (l. 9) 4		e (l. 41) 1	
c (l. 33) 6		f (l. 69) 3	

3 Ask students to underline or make a note of the parts of the text where they found the answers to the questions.

Suggested answers

a They are an advertising hoax – neither they, nor the website that's advertising them, actually exist.

b Asimov's stories were more imaginative and based on science, whereas his contemporaries followed an existing formula.

c It would be very difficult to programme robots to obey the three laws, and, even then, simply programming them would not be sufficient to control their actions.

d To show that Asimov's first law is self-contradictory.

e That we ought to take them seriously and do more research.

After students have found the answers, point out that these questions summarise the main parts of the text.

4 Point out that the multiple-choice questions are the same as the questions in exercise 3, and that if they have answered these correctly they should be able to choose the correct answers for 1–5. Emphasise the information in the *Tip* box: that it can help to try to answer the questions by looking at the stems only first. It should then be possible to eliminate any obviously wrong options, and focus carefully on whether all the information in the remaining options is accurate and relevant.

Key

1 C   2 D   3 A   4 B   5 D

5 Refer students back to the text for any ideas to support their points of view.

Vocabulary p96

1 If students have access to dictionaries encourage them to check the differences in meaning. Where possible, ask them to think of any real examples to support their answers.

Key

a too many people

b *famine*: when food supplies runs out, often as a result of drought.
drought: when there is a severe lack of water.

c *natural resource*: examples include oil, water, coal.
financial resource: a supply of money.

d *volcano* (a *tornado* is a violent windstorm with a funnel-shaped cloud)

e *landslide* (a *flood* is the rising of water onto normally dry land)

f *earthquake* (a *tremor* is a very small earthquake)

g *contagious* (meaning it passes easily from one person to another; *controversial* refers to something that people disagree about)

2 **Key**

1 a vital
  b trivial
2 a critical
  b controversial
3 a momentary
  b momentous
4 a principal
  b principle
5 a antisocial
  b unsocial

Optional activity

Students look up the words in their dictionaries and make a note of other meanings and collocations, e.g. *vital*: lively, energetic, critical; issue.

Grammar p96

1 Ask students to look back to the Lead in on page 93 to see if they can summarise some of their own or the speakers' views using conditional clauses beginning with *If*.

Key

a 3   b 4   c 2   d 1

2 Key

a I'd give up, I had
b would have found, hadn't managed
c stay out, will probably kill
d I'd realised, would have bought
e you leave, rust
f wouldn't have crashed, hadn't run out

3 Key

1 a The speaker knows you are having problems.
  b If in the near future you find it difficult the speaker will help.
2 a *could* expresses possibility.
  b *would* expresses certainty.
3 a is less formal than b).
4 a The condition is possible.
  b The speaker knows you are not staying and there is a tone of regret.
5 b is more formal than a).

4 After completing the exercises, point out the inversion in f) and ask students if it makes the first part of the clause more or less emphatic (more). Ask them to rewrite it as an *If* clause, i.e. *If the manager were to find out …*

Key

a hadn't tied him, wouldn't have ended up
b are looking, go
c fade, leave
d want, try
e would have arrived, hadn't been digging
f Were, would be

6 Key

a unless (replace with *without*)
b provided
c as long as (replace with *Supposing*)
d supposing (replace with *as long as/provided*)
e provided (replace with *unless*)
f as long as
g unless

Optional activity

Ask students to rephrase sentences a–g using an *if* clause for each one.

a They would have ended up divorced if their friends hadn't intervened.
b I'll marry you if you don't expect me to get on with your mother!
c If you won the lottery, how would you spend the money?
d Jim will be allowed out of prison if he reports to the police station twice a week.
e Tonight's open-air concert will be cancelled if the weather doesn't improve.
f I'll be raring to go tomorrow if I get a good night's sleep tonight.
g There's no hope of our team winning the League if we don't start to play better.

7 Ask students to read through the paragraph first and check the meaning of *kicked out, bone idle, on the cards, drifted in and out* and *urge*.

Key

1 had told
2 would never have believed
3 had
4 did/would do
5 paid
6 wouldn't get
7 had
8 was/were
9 might earn
10 hadn't urged
11 would never have got
12 would still be working

Listening p98

1 Ask students to talk about any voluntary work they have done.

Suggested answers

a developing countries, e.g. in Africa or Asia
b money, fresh water, food, shelter, medical supplies, clothing, equipment, etc.
c medical, educational, engineering, construction, planning, etc.
d Volunteers may be able to give immediate help to save or improve lives in disaster zones, or may be able to implement techniques and training that will have long-term benefits. Volunteers will also have the opportunity to learn about a new culture and people, learn a new language, etc.

2 Tell students to read through the questions and options before they listen. Remind them to listen to the whole of each corresponding section carefully before they make their final decision.

Key

1 B 2 C 3 D 4 C 5 A 6 B

Tapescript

Interviewer: Today we have in the studio Tom Davies, who has recently returned from a year's stint working as a volunteer in Nepal. Tom, welcome.

Tom: Hi!

Interviewer: Now what originally motivated you to take a year out and spend that time living and working in what to most people would be a rather isolated part of the world?

Tom: Well, I suppose I'd been thinking about doing something of the kind for quite a long time, actually. **I felt that I should be trying to put something back into the world**, rather than just keep on taking what I wanted from it. Anyway, one day, I picked up a newspaper that someone had left on the train, and I saw this advert. In the blurb, it said something like 'volunteers return to their own country equipped with invaluable professional experience, a wealth of memories, and a whole new perspective on life'. I decided that it was the job for me.

Interviewer: But it must have been difficult leaving family and friends behind for that length of time.

Tom: Of course it was. But as far as I'm concerned, when you're young, you don't dwell on things like that. You look upon life as a bit of an adventure and **you tend to think, 'A year – it'll be over in no time at all.'** And it was, in a funny sort of a way. Plus the fact that it was so far away, there's no way I could just nip back home for the odd weekend. As it turned out, I was so busy that I don't think I would have had time to do that anyway. Much better to take advantage of my free time to explore my surroundings, which I did to the full.

Interviewer: Now, for those listeners who know very little about the organisation you were working for – is the work really voluntary?

Tom: In as much as you're not paid a salary, yes, it is. But that doesn't mean that you're expected to live on nothing. There are lots of benefits on offer. You get a living allowance, accommodation, insurance and flights all paid for. You are also given individual training, support and advice before your departure. You have the chance to do some networking with other volunteers, too. **But what clinched it for me was the fact that when you come back to your own country, you get additional support in the form of grants and advice to help you settle back in.**

Interviewer: And did you have any choice in what kind of placement you were given?

Tom: Oh, absolutely. There were no nasty shocks in that respect! I was a volunteer in Nepal with an organisation which aimed to achieve conservation through human development. This was right up my street! While a colleague (who later became my best mate) and I were working there, we developed our own programme – it was a real challenge! Our aims were twofold: one was to reduce the numbers of snow leopards lost because of illegal hunting. But, at the same time, we set out to increase incomes and opportunities for the local communities living in the area.

Interviewer: That sounds like a tall order!

Tom: Indeed. **Snow leopards are a flagship species** for bio-diversity in the Himalayas, and they're one of the world's most endangered cat species. Hunting them is prohibited, but residents view them as a pest because they kill large numbers of livestock each year.

Interviewer: And how did your programme help tackle these difficulties?

Tom: Well, we tackled both issues simultaneously by introducing livestock insurance for farmers, and also through the creation of savings and credit groups. The two projects were deliberately linked **to allow profits from the savings credits groups to be used in compensation for livestock losses.** Donors provided the initial grant and funding for the project but the project itself is owned and run by the local community. This means that the scheme is self-financing, and the community makes the decisions. Local people can now borrow money to develop business or enterprises.

Interviewer: Can you give us an example?

Tom: Certainly. One that springs to mind was the purchase of cheese-making equipment. Local milk is now converted into cheese to be sold to trekkers who pass through the area. We hope all this will ultimately help the snow leopard. But **at the moment it's difficult to determine if there has been a decrease in the number of snow leopard deaths due to poaching**, but what we can say for certain is that many of the herders have started to insure their herd against loss. What we are counting on is that profits from the scheme can be put back into community projects and veterinary services, which will benefit the whole region.

Interviewer: And your own plans for the future?

Tom: No more travelling for me for a while, that's for sure – unless it's on holiday. I've done what I set out to do and I'm more than happy with that – but I wouldn't have missed it for the world!

Interviewer: Tom, that's all we've got time for, I'm afraid, so thank you …

Speaking p99

1 Ask students to give each picture a general heading and brainstorm any ideas they have before moving on to task 2, e.g. 1 housing, 2 career/studies, etc.

2 Make sure students are clear what the choices represented are:
1 type of acccommodation
2 work or study
3 type of car
4 small or big family
5 what to eat/preferred diet
6 choice of holiday type or destination

Remind students to discuss as many pictures and issues as possible in four minutes and to answer both question prompts, giving reasons for their ideas.

3 Key
1 c appropriate
2 a appropriate
3 a too short but good vocabulary (*make up my mind*)
4 c doesn't really answer the question
5 b appropriate
6 b First part of the answer is suitable but the candidate seems to have misunderstood the question and gives a rather confusing answer.

Tapescript

1 It's something that influences everything we do. After all, if we really can't afford to do something, then there's very little point wasting time wondering whether to do it or not.
2 Probably very trivial everyday decisions. Really important ones are usually much easier to make because there's so much at stake – so you think about them in a more logical way. They're not made on the spur of the moment.
3 It's easy for me to make up my mind.
4 I am very interested in money. I would like to be very rich one day. I would like to buy lots of houses and cars.
5 I would say that some maybe not so important ones we do make entirely on our own and we have the freedom to choose. But others are influenced by friends, family, people at work – or just circumstances in general.
6 That's an interesting question! Yes, there are plenty of opportunities to make a decision. I agree with them.

4 Check students understand the meaning of all the phrases and perhaps ask them to give synonyms.

Suggested answers

at stake – at risk/in danger
in the long run – eventually
on the spur of the moment – spontaneously, unplanned
short term – in the immediate future
out of the blue – unexpectedly
out of our control – out of our hands/not in our power

There is authentic practice of this section on page 95 of the Workbook.

Use of English p100

2 Ask students to find example sentences to support their answer, e.g. the final sentence.

Key
b

3 Remind students to pay attention to any dependent prepositions or grammatical structures which follow the missing word (infinitive with or without *to*, gerund, tenses, etc.). Tell them to think carefully about subtle differences in meaning between the choices. Students could check this in their dictionary.

Key

1 D   2 B   3 A   4 D   5 C   6 A   7 B   8 A   9 C
10 B   11 D   12 D

When they have completed the text and checked their answers, ask students to summarise the writer's argument and say to what extent they agree with it.

Vocabulary p101

1 Refer students back to the text on page 100 and check the meaning of the phrase *a means to an end* following gap 7 (something done to achieve something else). Ask them to read through the sentences quickly to see which of a–h this expression fits into (c), before doing the rest of the exercise.

Key

a	loose	d	meet	g	in
b	sight	e	up	h	on
c	means	f	at		

2 Students should be able to find the expressions more easily either under head words like *means* or by checking under *end* for set expressions.

3

Key

a   in the end (g)
b   be at a loose end (a)
c   there's no end in sight (b)
d   ended up (e)
e   at the end (f)
f   on end (h)
g   make ends meet (d)
h   a means to an end (c)

Writing p101

1 Students may have more than one answer for each category. Encourage them to explain which words may fall into different categories and why, e.g. *single* relates to relationship, but it may also relate to the type of lifestyle you choose. Ask students which categories they think include some of the most difficult decisions.

Suggested answers

a   5, 6, 13
b   6, 10, 12
c   1, 2, 7, 8, 11, 14, 15
d   4, 8, 11, 13, 14, 15
e   1, 2, 3, 4, 9, 10, 13

2 Remind students that it is important to consider who your target audience is, as this will help you decide on the appropriate register for your writing.

Key

a They focus on the choice between work versus study.

b B is more appropriate because it starts in an interesting way by drawing in the reader with some questions. The style is informal and lively, which would probably attract the attention of a younger audience and is more appropriate for a magazine than A.

3 Refer students to the Writing Guide to check their ideas.

Key

c

4 Check students understand the meaning of some of the less formal expressions, e.g. *it's up to you*, *been in your shoes*, *think things through*. Elicit that the inappropriate choices are too formal.

Key

b, c, d, e, h

5 Ask students to compare answers in pairs or groups. They should be able to suggest various ways of rephrasing the information. This is useful practice for English in Use Register Transfer.

Suggested answers

a Don't make a decision between work or study until you've thought about it long and hard.

f Take advantage of/Make the most of facilities in your neighbourhood/what's on your doorstep, like your local library.

g Don't put off your decision for so long that you leave yourself with no choices/it's too late to make one.

6 Check students understand any difficult vocabulary in the text, e.g. *branch out on your own*, *cramp your style*, *plain sailing*, *foot the bills*, *savour your independence*. Make sure they check the complete text for sense and structure.

Key

1 e   2 c   3 h   4 d   5 g   6 a   7 f   8 b

7 Draw students' attention to the question in the introduction which gets the reader's attention and to the fact that the writer weighs up all sides of the argument in the following paragraphs.

Key

a When to leave home and become independent.

b The economic consequences of moving out from home/practicalities of location.

c By giving examples for each point.

d To give advice and to make the reader think about both sides of the argument.

For an assessed authentic answer to this Writing task, see page 13 of the *Writing and Speaking Assessment Booklet* in the Teacher's Pack.

Review p104

1 Key

a landslide
b natural resource
c famine
d tornado
e contagious disease
f over-populated

2 Key

a term
b run
c stake
d spur
e blue
f control

3 Key

a momentary
b controversial
c trivial
d momentous
e unsocial
f principal
g antisocial

4 Key

a at a loose end
b there's no end in sight
c make ends meet
d at the end
e a means to an end
f ended up
g in the end
h on end

5 Key

1 consider
2 make
3 against
4 mind
5 Weigh
6 to

It's a crime

Lead in p105

1 Tell students to use the context to work out the meaning of the six items before using a dictionary if necessary. Check pronunciation. Elicit the meaning of any other difficult vocabulary, e.g. *peaked*, *offender*, *acquaintance*, again encouraging students to use the context to help.

Key

criminal damage: damage to property
counterfeit: fake/imitation
robbery: take something illegally, e.g. money, a-car,-etc.
domestic violence: physical/emotional violence to a family member. In most cases this is towards women or children.
mugging: attacking someone, usually in the street and taking something from them illegally.
fraud: cheating/deceiving

Ask students if they can remember and tell any crime stories that have recently appeared in the press, using some of the language items.

2 Suggested answers

b Falling crime statistics may reflect a real drop in criminal incidents due to better policing, better personal security, higher employment (and therefore fewer criminals), or may simply reflect a decrease in reported crimes, perhaps due to unwillingness to do so on the part of the victims.

Reading p106

1 Encourage students to think of recent films they have seen or books they have read that are about crimes. They could work in pairs or small groups then compare answers with other students.

Suggested answers

An interesting setting, convincing characters, a gripping story, an element of mystery to keep the reader guessing, an element of surprise, a twist in the tail, a fight between 'good and evil', some 'juicy' crimes, etc.

2 You might like to do the first section as a timed activity with the whole class and agree on a heading before students continue with the other sections. Encourage students to read within the set time limit and ignore unknown words. Elicit why this is a useful exercise (by identifying the general theme of each paragraph they should be able to locate the items in the exam task more quickly).

Suggested answers

a The key elements of crime fiction.
b Using other authors as a model.
c Choosing your main characters.
d Choosing your crime.
e Making your criminal convincing.
f Engaging the reader.

3 Encourage students to follow the advice in the *Tip* box. None of the questions will focus on the same piece of information in the text, so once students have identified which part of the text answers a particular question, they should not need to read that specific part again, although they may still need to understand the overall context it contributes to.

Key

1 E   2 D/E   3 D/E   4 A   5 B/F   6 B/F   7 B
8 D   9 C   10 D   11 A   12 E   13 B

Optional activity

Divide students into three groups and ask them to find the following words in the text. They should decide what part of speech they are, and work out or check their meanings in a dictionary, before explaining them to the class as a whole.

Group A

mislead (l. 7) *(v deceive)*
audacity (l. 20) *(n boldness)*
folly (l. 22) *(n stupidity)*
sloppy (l. 32) *(adj careless)*
twist (l. 37) *(n unexpected change)*

Group B

mutter (l. 41) *(v complain quietly)*
libel (l. 50) *(v wrongly accuse, damaging someone's reputation)*
enhance (l. 57) *(v improve)*
humdrum (l. 61) *(n normal and boring)*
blunt (l. 81) *(adj not sharp)*

Group C

spin a yarn (l. 91) *(phr tell a story)*
boil down to (l. 105) *(phr. come to one main point)*
wary (l. 124) *(adj careful)*
come up to scratch (l. 127) *(phr be good enough)*
cringe (l. 130) *(v feel afraid)*

4 Key

a of (l. 108)	d of (l. 103)	g of (l. 114)
b of (l. 98)	e for (l. 88)	h for (l. 122)
c of (l. 28)	f for (l. 76)	

5 Encourage students to think of films as well as books and to compare how different criminals and detectives are portrayed. They may like to consider the relationship between the criminal and detective and the way 'good and evil' are depicted. For those who don't like crime fiction, find out what it is that they don't like about it.

Vocabulary p108

1 After students have done the exercise, ask them to rank the crimes in order of seriousness and compare with other students. If they need help refer them back to page 105.

Key

a *manslaughter* is accidental or in self-defence; *murder* is deliberate or 'premeditated'
b *mugging* means to attack someone with intent to rob, usually in the street; *smuggling* means taking goods illegally from one place to another
c *bribery* means offering someone an illegal incentive to do something; *blackmail* means to threaten or intimidate someone for illegal purposes
d *burglary* means to enter a house illegally and rob; *robbery* means to take something illegally from a place or person (*rob someone of something*) and is often used with references to banks, etc.
e *arson* means to deliberately set fire to something; *assault* means to attack someone violently
f *fraud* means to deceive or cheat; *forgery* means to produce false documents for illegal purposes

2 Key

a mugger, mugging	d murder, murderer
b robber, robbery	e theft
c burgle, burglary	

3 Ask students to write sentences to illustrate the meaning of the words and expressions and compare with others, e.g. My brother does whatever he likes and <u>gets away with murder</u>.

4 Check the meaning of any difficult vocabulary, e.g. *caution, custody, tried, jury verdict, parole*. Older students may have done jury service and will be able to talk more about the process.

Key

1	for	4	of	6	to
2	with	5	against	7	on
3	into				

Grammar p108

1 After students have done the exercise, ask them to find any examples of passive structures in the text on page 106–107 (l. 7, l. 42, l. 45, l. 48/9, l. 72, l.78, etc.)

Key

a were appalled/is to be axed/are said to be
b could be colonised
c are being broken
d to be hosted
e can be made
f will have to be made
g are required

2 Refer students to the Grammar Reference if necessary.

Key

a *to be*, past   b subject   c by

3 Key

a a, c, e
b g
c f

4 Remind students that the passive tense is used more in written forms of text and that newspapers tend to include the passive frequently in reports and stories. Check students understand *well, quarried, bog site.*

Key

1 A 2,000-year-old shoe has recently been discovered
2 it has been kept damp
3 a lot more work needs to be done
4 Nothing like this has ever been found
5 everything is known
6 Similar shoes have been found
7 It may have been placed
8 it could have been simply lost
9 shoes were often buried

Optional activity

Ask students to find articles in English language magazines or newspapers to bring to class, to look at examples of passive forms. They could practise changing these into the active where possible and appropriate, and discuss the effect this has on the language.

5 Refer students to the second column of page 170 in the Grammar Reference and the section on *see, hear, make* and *allow* before they do exercises 5 and 6.

Key

a In a crackdown on antisocial behaviour, teenagers are being made to remove neighbourhood graffiti.
b The politician was heard to say under his breath that 'all journalists were troublemakers'.
c No one was allowed into the building until it was said to be safe.
d On the CCTV footage, money was clearly seen to change hands in return for a small package.

7 Refer students to page 171 in the Grammar Reference and the section on *have/get something done* before they do the exercise.

Suggested answers

a They should have/get the pipes fixed/repaired. Why don't they have/get the pipes fixed/repaired?
b You should have/get them taken up. I suggest you have/get them taken up.
c You should have/get it examined/looked at by a vet.
d You ought to have/get it re-decorated. How about having/getting it re-decorated?
e She should have/get it checked at the garage. I suggest she has/gets it checked at the garage.

8 Refer students to the bottom left-hand column of Grammar Reference page 170 for examples of these verbs in news reports before they do the exercise.

Key

a A UFO is rumoured to have crashed in Texas.
b Robbie Williams is said to be going to do another world tour.
c Scientists are believed to have found a new planet.
d Factory bosses are thought to be planning to make two hundred employees redundant.
e The event is assumed to have been cancelled because of the singer's poor health.

Listening p110

2 Once students have read the questions, refer them to the *tip* box to predict whether they are listening for more specific information or inferring, e.g. specific information: 1, 2, 4, inferring: 3, 5, 6.

Key

1 B   2 C   3 A   4 B   5 B   6 A

Optional activity

Ask students to discuss their opinions about extract 3.

Background information

The Millennium Dome is situated on the south bank of the Thames in London. The dome is the world's largest single-roofed structure, and was built to house a collection of exhibitions about Britain in the year 2000. It was renamed 'The O_2' in 2005.

Tapescript

Extract 1

A: In your book, you talk about some very entertaining robberies. Do you have a favourite?

B: Oh, yes! It happened at the Millennium Dome in London. The attempt was simple but daring, and a bit like a James Bond film.

A: Remind me what happened.

B: Well, a gang of criminals had been conspiring for months to steal the millennium jewels, which were on display there. **The plan was to smash their way in with a bulldozer, break through the security glass at the display, and snatch a dozen rare and valuable diamonds, including the Millennium Star.** The men behind the raid were well-known criminals and the police had had the ringleader under surveillance for some time. So the police decided to waited for them overnight.

A: Very clever!

B: Yes. The plan went ahead – the thieves crashed through the perimeter fence and into the Dome. But as they reached in to grab their prize, they found themselves well and truly cornered. Officers disguised as cleaners ordered the men to raise their hands and **they were caught red-handed.**

A: What a story, now …

Extract 2

A: Could we just run-through what happened?

B: I'd just booked into a hotel and I'd left my credit card details to guarantee payment. I'd only been in my room a few minutes when the phone rang. Apparently the credit card company had refused to authorise the card. I rang the company immediately and they said I'd overspent on my credit limit. They said I'd spend hundreds on sports equipment!

A: And you still had your credit card?

B: I certainly did. **That's what really got to me. How can anyone use your credit card if it's still in your possession?**

A: Very easily. What can happen is that when you pay for something, say in a restaurant, someone copies the card – clone it, if you like.

B: But what about PIN numbers? Nobody would be able to use the card.

A: Unfortunately payments can be made over the phone without your PIN number.

B: So does that mean I'm liable for all these bills?

A: Probably not. **It's fraud and credit card companies cover that possibility.** You've reported it to us and we take these matters seriously.

Extract 3

A: So, what exactly are you saying? Violent criminals should be allowed to walk free after a few years in prison?

B: Not at all. What I'm saying is that we have to rethink our attitudes towards crime and punishment. Years ago people thought that if you were made to pay for what you'd done – sent to prison – you'd be a better person when you came out. In fact, the opposite seems to be true. **A huge percentage of prisoners re-offend in the first few weeks after getting out.**

A: **Yes, I can see that something has to be done to prevent that.** But it's much better to consider punishments like community service for non-violent offenders.

B: Obviously, there's a difference between the types of criminal you're dealing with. But what we have to realise is that prisons are grossly overcrowded. So what **we have to come up with is a way of helping prisoners make a useful contribution to the world we live in and making the whole thing more positive.** We simply don't have room to house offenders.

Speaking p110

1 Key

They are all connected with things you are not allowed to do/are prohibited from doing.

2 Key

A refers to places which have special regulations
B refers to the reasons for the regulations being in place
C refers to possible consequences of breaking those regulations

Set 1 left-hand photo: a department store/to prevent damage to goods/being asked to leave the premises or having your property (food) removed
Set 1 right-hand photo: a quiet environment/to prevent interruption/having your property removed or being asked to leave the premises
Set 2 left-hand photo: a controlled parking zone/to avoid congestion/having to pay a fine
Set 2 right-hand photo: an airport check-in queue/to protect passengers and crew/having to pay a fine
Set 3 left-hand photo: a hard hat area/to prevent accident or injury/being sacked or being given a verbal warning or being asked to leave the premises or receiving a warning letter
Set 3 right-hand photo: a smoke-free environment/to maintain a healthy atmosphere/being asked to leave the premises

3 Refer students to the *tip* boxes and remind them that the prompts are there to help them focus on the task. Allow about a minute for each student.

4 Students don't necessarily have to agree with each other. Remind them to give reasons for their opinions.

Use of English p112

1 Ask students if they have to carry identity cards in their country and if they think they are necessary and why. Ask what they think about the fact that some countries do not currently have them, e.g. the UK. With more mature students you could encourage a discussion on whether national security or personal freedom is more important.

2 As students read quickly, they could compare the ideas in the text with any points they made in exercise 1.

Key

security cameras, 'national facial recognition system', availability of financial details to various companies.

3 Explain to students that the aim of this task is to make them think carefully about the difference between words with similar meanings. If, when brainstorming possible answers, they can think of more than one answer, it is probable that only one fits the meaning and the structure of the sentence. Sometimes there may be more than one correct answer.

Key

1	as	6	that	11	without
2	it	7	on	12	no
3	like	8	more	13	to
4	into	9	being	14	if
5	between	10	from	15	not

Vocabulary p113

1 Before students complete the sentences, ask them to give a definition for each phrasal verb in context.

Suggested answers

a The last album; … was the best they have ever made.
b the fact; … have been complete luck as I didn't study much.
c no object; … see what was wrong.
d these figures; … they don't seem to add up.
e the lights; … everyone fell asleep.

2 If students find this difficult, do one or two examples as a whole class first. Ask them to think of another verb which would fit into each gap before they try to complete them with the phrasal verb.

Key

a	gave	c	check	e	get
b	set	d	hold	f	worked

3 Key

give out f, i
check out c, j
hold out b, d
get out g, h
work out e, a

Optional activity

Elicit sentences to show students have understood the use of the phrasal verbs in exercise 3 with an object.

Suggested answers

a I can't work out the answer to this sum without a calculator.
d The taxi driver held out his hand waiting for a tip.
h One of the policeman got out his gun and threatened to shoot.
i They were giving out free samples of coffee at the supermarket today.
j If you go to New York, you must check out the fabulous nightlife.

4

Ask students to complete each sentence in two different ways, once with and once without an object.

Suggested answers

a ... my mobile phone and rang the police immediately.
... of the building as quickly as I could.
b ... by 12 noon.
... their excellent rooftop restaurant.
c ... for eight hours in order to see their favourite stars.
... autograph books for their favourite stars to sign.

Writing p114

1

Students could add any other ideas they think would be useful for report writing and then compare their ideas with the Writing Guide.

Key

d, e

2

Remind students of the importance of reading through all the information carefully and including all points outlined in the task. Suggest they think of a suitable title and paragraph headings for the report, e.g.
- Report on Murder Mystery Weekend trip to Edinburgh
- Introduction
- Positive aspects
- Negative aspects
- Recommendations

Suggested answers

The writer includes all the points mentioned in the timetable notes, but the tone is often too informal. The opening of the report is unsuitable (it isn't a formal letter). It should have a title. The introduction does state the purpose of the report but the writer should be careful not too lift too many phrases direct from the input text.
It is a good idea to try and give each paragraph a clear heading.

Background information

Edinburgh is the capital city of Scotland. It is situated on the east coast and is the annual venue for the Edinburgh Festival, the largest performing arts festival in the world.

3

When students have completed the task you could ask them to suggest any other phrases for introducing and concluding reports, before referring them to the Writing Guide.

Key

a of b In c up d to e into f On

Introduction: a, d
Conclusion: b, c, e, f

4 Key

a, d and f are not appropriate as they are informal. Check students know what structures follow the appropriate phrases, e.g.

b I'd like to suggest (that) you improve the facilities.

c It might be a good idea to fly to Edinburgh. It might be a good idea if you provided more time for the visit.

e You could consider starting the trip later.

g One possible solution would be to shorten the tour.
One possible solution would be flying back to London the following day.

5 Encourage students to include some of the language from exercises 3 and 4 in their report.

For an assessed authentic answer to this Writing task, see page 14 of the *Writing and Speaking Assessment Booklet* in the Teacher's Pack.

Review p116

1 Key

a of 3	d of 2	g for 4
b for 1	e of 6	h of 8
c for 5	f of 7	

2 Key

1 c, e, j, l
2 b, d, f, g, h, i, k, l, m
3 a

3 Key

a 3 b 5 c 1 d 7 e 6 f 4 g 2

4 Key

a pulled over	e hold on	i held out
b worked out	f put out	j check out
c set out	g set out	k gave out
d bring out	h get over	l work out

5 Key

a of b to c up d In e On f into

6 Key

1 There	5 with	8 In addition
2 to	6 so	9 all
3 being	7 worse	10 help
4 problems		

Buying and selling

10

Lead in p117

1 Ask students to look quickly at the photos and decide what ways of buying and selling they can see.

Suggested answers
an auction, a street market, the internet, a charity shop

3 If you have students of different age groups, ask them to compare their lists and see if priorities are different. Ask them to add any other things they regularly spend money on.

4 Younger students may receive allowances or pocket money. Find out whether they consider it a good idea or not to be given money by their parents. For c), students might like to discuss whether adverts usually persuade us more with visuals or with words.

Reading p118

1 To answer both parts of the question students need to read the main text and the missing paragraphs, so you might like to divide up the class and have half read each section and then report back.

Key
eBay was started by Pierre Omidyar in 1995 after he sold a broken laser pointer on the Internet.
The writer bought a vintage Soviet Union cycling jersey.

2 Encourage students to use the context to work out the meanings of the words first, before checking in a dictionary if necessary.

Key
a reports by newspapers/the press
b large businesses
c products that are no longer being sold
d people who set up a commercial enterprise which does well
e improving your work status

3 Remind students to look for key words and phrases which help them make links between paragraphs.

Key
1 C   2 G   3 B   4 D   5 A   6 F
Paragraph E is not needed.

Vocabulary p120

1 Key
a in (ready to begin)
b of (nothing to do with you/not your concern)
c on (travelling for work)
d out (stopped trading)
e to (begin)

2 Check students understand *haggle*, if it didn't arise when doing the exercises on page 117. Students may confuse *receipt* with *recipe* or *prescription*.

Key
a ✓
b try and get a lower price for something
c buy a lot of often unnecessary things
d ✓
e ✓
f ✓
g a compulsive shopper
h ✓

Optional activity

Ask students to look back at the text on pages 118–119 to find other expressions connected with buying and selling, e.g.
pick up a bargain (l. 9)
make a few quid (l. 10)
money-making possibilities (l. 54)
be up for sale (l. 66)

Grammar p120

1 Remind students that although they are accustomed to studying conditional tenses under the headings of zero, first, second and third conditional, there are also mixed forms and that the time reference in each part of the clause affects the tense used. Tell students to pay attention to any time references in the sentences, e.g. *now*, *this year*, etc.

Key
a wouldn't be, had listened
b hadn't lent, wouldn't be living
c I'd be, hadn't been
d didn't have to, would (have) come

e wouldn't have misread, wasn't, weren't
f didn't listen, weren't listening, will have

2 Ask students to work in pairs or small groups and then compare ideas as a whole class.

Suggested answers
a ... we hadn't invented satellites.
b ... we would still be sending most correspondence by post.
c ... it is possible that there isn't any/we probably never will.
d ... I had saved more money in the last few years.
e ... it didn't have such beautiful old monuments.

3 Key
a ✓
b would propose
c was/were a bit easier
d ✓
e could afford
f would stop

4 Key
a sentence a
b *would*, sentences b and f
c *could*, sentence e
d past perfect simple, sentence d

6 Refer students to the section on *Wishes and regrets* on page 180 in the Grammar Reference before they do the exercise. Point out that *do* in b is used for emphasis because the speaker is angry.

Key
a didn't have to/wasn't going (*could* if you hate football!)
b would listen
c hadn't given
d had told
e would come out/shine/was shining
f weren't
g didn't have
h lived
i could
j hadn't eaten
k would happen

7 Before students complete the exercise, ask them to discuss whether they had any particular wishes or dreams as a child and if any of them came true.

Key

1	was able to/could	7	will go
2	had	8	hadn't been
3	would be	9	may never have picked
4	had stayed	10	applied
5	would happen	11	would start
6	continue		

Listening p122

1 Ask students where we usually see adverts and which they think are most effective. Refer them to the photos on pages 122–3 for ideas but without going into too much detail.

2 Key

1 D   2 B   3 C   4 A   5 A   6 D

Tapescript

Interviewer: Paula, welcome to the studio today. Now you run what is considered by those who know what they're talking about to be a very successful advertising agency. What inspired you to enter the world of advertising?

Paula: I'm not sure if I know the answer to that but I suppose I've always been a bit of an entrepreneur – not the ruthless kind, of course! I'm certainly not very artistic – never have been – but I have an eye for design. And although I've certainly never had the gift of the gab, **I can argue my way out of a corner, and get my own way!**

Interviewer: But success didn't come overnight, did it?

Paula: Not at all. But it hasn't all been hard grind. I started at the bottom and **gradually worked my way up**, but I can't say I didn't enjoy it along the way. **I've had my ups and a few downs, too.** But in this field, you've just got to pick yourself up and start all over again!

Interviewer: How would you say that the world of advertising compares to working in other fields?

Paula: Working in advertising's certainly tougher, make no mistake. It's often said in advertising that you're only as good as your last idea. **In reality, you're only as good as your next one.** Our business is different because it constantly has to break with the past. This need for reinvention obviously affects the industry's culture. There can be very few industries that are expected to have a new idea every day.

Interviewer: But is there any evidence to back up what you are saying?

Paula: There's plenty of proof that you can't rely on past achievements! A quick glance at advertising shows that the industry is littered with **campaigns that stayed around too long and ended up damaging the brand.** So much so that the brand often disappears for ever – a problem one famous and highly successful fashion company encountered in its last campaign.

Interviewer: So what steps can you take to ensure your long-term survival?

Paula: Well, the only way to 'ensure your long-term survival' as you so aptly put it, is relentless investment in talent and opportunity, and **a constant questioning of one's past – the desire to break with what you've created and the courage to start again** – the 'If it worked yesterday, it certainly won't work tomorrow' sort of philosophy. For example, for most brands, the general thinking is that a strong heritage is considered an asset, a competitive advantage. And on the surface, there doesn't seem anything wrong with that! But it's the conventional view and it presents advertising agencies with an interesting dilemma. How do they succeed as brands? We are, perhaps, an industry that can be trapped by our past glory. Just as a shark has to keep swimming to survive, an agency has to keep evolving to succeed. It has no fixed assets, no past equity to trade, and in reality, very little goodwill.

Interviewer: So all in all, would you recommend the industry as a career?

Paula: Overall, I would say it's an industry for newcomers. It's an environment where the newcomer is regarded with greater relevance than anything else. And this is probably because **as an industry we're obsessed with youth. A 50-year-old creative is an increasing rarity.** Or if they're still employed, they are consigned to some branch office in the back of beyond. We're in an industry where, for good or bad, history is suspect and the future is the prize. Of course, any business has to look to tomorrow, expecially in facing today's relentless competition. But advertising must uniquely be an industry that has to forget about its past in order to ensure its future!

Interviewer: Paula, thanks for talking to us today. And now …

3 Elicit the opposite of each of the four adjectives (*illegal, indecent, dishonest, untruthful*) and ask how, in gerneral terms, adverts might be each of these things. Elicit the subtle difference in meaning between *honest* (being genuine and telling the whole truth) and *truthful* (being factually true, i.e. not a lie). Ask why it is important that adverts shoud have these qualities, and for speicific examples of any that have been banned, and why.

Speaking p123

1 Check that students know the names for the different types of advertising, especially *advertising hoardings* (2), *sandwich board* (5), *leaflet* (6), *junk mail* (7).

Suggested answers
1 radio, magazines
2 most expensive: radio adverts
   least expensive: sandwich board on the street
3 junk mail, leaflets
4 advertising hoardings

2 Key

a 2 (A)   b 2 (B)   c 1 (B)   d 4 (B)   e 3 (A)
f 3 (B)

Tapescript

1 A I don't think an ad on the radio would be very effective.
  B That's rubbish. It's a very good idea.
2 A This isn't a very effective way of advertising anything. Nobody reads what's on a board like this, or even remembers what product's being advertised, do they?
  B Er … no.
3 A This – how is this called in English?
  B Oh, it's called junk mail, I think – things that you don't want that come through your letter box.
4 A If you ask me, advertising in a magazine is an excellent way of reaching a large section of the public.
  B It's expensive but you're right. I'm sure it pays off.

3 Monitor students to check they are discussing all the photos first and expanding on their ideas before deciding on the best two for the promotion. Make sure they keep to the time limit of four minutes.

4 You could extend the task by asking students to think of another two or three questions related to the topic, e.g. *Do you think there should be some TV channels that have no advertising? What stereotypes of people are often portrayed in adverts?*

Use of English p124

1 Ask students to suggest adjectives to describe the image presented in the photos, e.g. *flashy, over the top*. Ask them if they know what sort of music this is associated with (hip-hop) and what fashions are associated with other types of music.

2 Remind students to always read the text once quickly, ignoring the mistakes, to get a general idea of its content.

Key

Hip-hop and R and B stars, and other celebrities. Even traditional jewellery companies are now making money from it.

3 Refer students to the *tip* box. Encourage them to check their answers in a dictionary, looking up the head word and consulting different parts of speech. Remind students to check spelling.

Key

1	unnoticed	6	increasingly
2	glamorous	7	incredible
3	surprising	8	feverishly
4	traditional	9	competition
5	unexpected	10	basic

4 Key

a	fierce	d	face
b	taste	e	keen
c	fact		

Vocabulary p125

1 Make sure students know where the word stress falls on each word:

a economic, economical

b personal, personnel

c alternative, alternate (but alternate as a verb)

d products, produce (but produce as a verb)

e opportunities, possibilities

Key

a economic   c alternate   e opportunities
b personnel   d produce

2 **Key**

a personal   c possibilities   e alternative
b products   d economical

Ask students to explain the difference in meaning between the pairs of words in exercise 1a–e.

> **Optional activity**
>
> Ask students to write an example sentence of their own for the words not used in a–e.

3 **Key**

1 scarcely   6 fairly
2 honesty   7 tirelessly
3 untrustworthy   8 environmentally
4 employees   9 really
5 sensitive   10 highly

Writing p126

1 Ask students if they would do any of the jobs shown in the photos giving reasons. Some students may have already done work experience if they are still studying at university, so encourage them to talk about whether the experience was useful or not.

2 Remind students to underline the key input points in the task, then check whether the writer of the model answer included all the points and how he organised them.

Key

- The writer worked for RPC music, one of the oldest record companies in the world.
- He worked in the publicity department helping with promotional literature and organising an interview, in the sales department checking stock and processing orders, and in the design department arranging photo shoots and designing a CD cover.
- The experience was generally positive, but he would have liked to spend more time there.

3 **Key**

Generally the answer is yes for a–e. The writer has used good, clear headings, fairly formal register, includes the main points and has used linking words (*On the whole, However, but*). The writer generally creates a good impression.

4 You could suggest that students do some research on the Internet if they have no previous work experience. If some students in class have had work experience, get them to work with others who haven't to plan and focus on main points. Stress the information in the *Tip* box about the importance of making a plan, so that students don't get halfway through writing an answer and realise they have run out of ideas.

5 You could ask students to add any other relevant points, e.g. working alone or in a team.

Suggested answers

Things to consider:

a number of hours in the day/week; start and finish time; whether any night or weekend work is involved; if overtime is paid; how the hours fit with your domestic and social life

b how far from home; how difficult or expensive to get to by public transport; if there are parking facilities; if it's close to shops and other facilities; if the site is attractive/pleasant/healthy to work in

c whether there is a canteen/restaurant on site or somewhere to buy/make drinks, etc.; older students may hope there is a crèche for their children; whether there is a shop on site, etc.

d whether staff are expected to dress smartly – all the time or only at certain times; whether there is a uniform and if so who pays for it

e if every day will be the same or if there is some variety; whether staff can move from one department to another; if you will be working with people doing similar jobs

For an assessed authentic answer to this Writing task, see page 15 of the *Writing and Speaking Assessment Booklet* in the Teacher's Pack.

Review p128

1 Key

1 out of business
2 on business
3 none of your business
4 in business
5 down to business

2 Key

a window shopping
b shopping spree
c shopaholic
d on credit
e haggle
f receipt
g shop around
f shoplift

3 Key

a opportunity
b economical

4 Key

a 4 b 7 c 1 d 9 e 3 f 2 g 5 h 10 i 8 j 6

5 Key

1 aim
2 assigned
3 set up
4 spent
5 on
6 make
7 benefit
8 period
9 hesitation

Entertainment or art?

Lead in p129

1 Ask students if there are any interesting or famous art galleries where they live and what kind of exhibits they have. Ask if they like the kinds of art shown, giving reasons. The pictures are:
1 *Face with two moods* (John Nelson)
2 detail from *Madonna in the Meadow* (Raphael)
3 *Queen Elizabeth II of the United Kingdom* (Andy Warhol)
4 head of *David* (Michelangelo)
5 Solaris Gregory in face paint by Tony Gregory

Reading p130

1 Ask students to briefly discuss in what situations people might *perform* in public and what difficulties there might be in doing this. Ask them to quickly read the first few lines of each extract to decide what kind of performance is mentioned and then read the whole extract.

Key
1 Performance art
2 Public speaking
3 Theatre performances

2 Refer students to the *tip* box and ask them to note down any difficult words or phrases to see if they can guess the meaning in context, e.g. *a nutter* in extract 1 is defined by the following description of behaviour and actions, which is unconventional.

Key
1 C   2 A   3 C   4 D   5 B   6 C

Vocabulary p132

1 Encourage students to check any unfamiliar words in dictionaries.

Key

a easel	d gallery	f palette
b canvas	e landscape	g watercolour
c sketch		

They are all connected with art and painting. The other groups are:

a films	d films	f films
b books	e theatre	g theatre
c music/songs		

2 Key

a canvas	c subtitles	e gallery
b lyrics	d plot	f rehearsal

3 You might want to divide the class up into pairs or small groups and ask them to look for at least two words not used in task 2. Students could then re-form as pairs/groups and teach/test each other.

4 Ask students to give examples to support their answers.

Suggested answers
c films with battle scenes (science-fiction/historical epics/war films, etc.) large crowd scenes or street scenes
e home entertainment has improved and therefore become more popular, smaller cinema audiences, DVDs give cheaper and higher-quality access to films at home, films can be downloaded from the Internet at low cost, similar changes in the music industry with downloading cheap, fast and of good quality, effects of piracy in film and music, etc.

Grammar p132

1

Key

a faster	f much hotter
b the more	g a great deal worse
c the most ancient	h more wrong
d as rigorous as	i older than me/I am
e the least convincing	

2 Key

a trickier	c wetter	e paler
b slimmer	d drier	

3

Put students into groups to do the exercise, then compare answers as a whole class. If they aren't sure of the answers encourage them to hypothesise, e.g. *I think it might/could/may be … because … .* Encourage them to use a range of structures, and remind them of the language for *Making decisions and giving reasons* on page 75.

Suggested answers

a Jupiter is the farthest/furthest from the Earth. Mars is nearer the Earth than Jupiter and Mars. Venus is nearer than Jupiter but further than Mars.
(Jupiter: 588 million km; Venus: 40 million km; Mars: 35 million km)

b The electric guitar is the oldest. The portable calculator is more recent than the transistor radio but not as recent as the calculator. The portable calculator is the most recent.
(electric guitar: 1930s; transistor radio: 1954; portable calculator: 1967)

c The Pacific Ocean is the largest. The Atlantic is larger than the Indian Ocean but not as large as the Pacific. The Indian Ocean is the smallest/smaller than the others.
(Pacific 165 760 000 sq. km; Atlantic 81 585 000 sq. km; Indian Ocean 73 556 000 sq. km)

d Chocolate has the most calories. Lettuce has the least calories. Bread has fewer calories than/not as many calories as chocolate but more than lettuce.
(100 g chocolate: 530 kcal; slice of white bread: 140 kcal; lettuce: 19 kcal)

4

Point out that all the words quantify the adjectives used in comparative and superlative statements.

Key

a 4   b 3   c 1   d 2

5 Key

a slightly	c slightly	e nowhere near
b far	d much	

6 Key

a far/much/a great deal/a lot
b nowhere near/nothing like
c just (nothing like)
d a great deal/a lot more
e a bit/slightly/a little

7

Before they do the exercise, refer students to page 181 of the Grammar Reference and the section on *Degree*, and remind them to think about the position of the words in italics in relation to the adjective.

Key

a so	d so	f too
b enough	e so	g so
c such		

8 Key

a as	c like	e like
b as	d as	

Listening p134

1 Many students will have probably seen a Pixar animated film, so may be able to identify the films the characters shown are from (*Nemo*, *The Incredibles*). If they have seen these films, ask what they thought of them and what elements of them would appeal to adults and to children.

2 Suggested answers

1	noun	5	adjective
2	adjective	6	noun
3	number	7	noun
4	noun	8	noun (plural)

3 Key

1	computer	5	realistic
2	puzzling	6	magic formula
3	17/seventeen	7	message
4	patience	8	jokes

Tapescript

Inside an office complex **near San Francisco, one of the 10 most powerful computers** in the world hums and blinks in a dark, glass chamber. Known as the Renderfarm, the computer represents the final stage in a Pixar movie. It takes the millions of equations that the studio's animators have created to control each character, and crunches them down into individual frames of film. Pixar are now one of the most successful film studios in the history of the cinema. But Pixar employees become visibly disturbed by the suggestion that sheer computing power might be the secret of, what is to their rivals, **their puzzling success**. In Hollywood, though, trying to figure out Pixar's secret has become a matter of panicky necessity. Since 1995, the company has had an unbroken record of triumphs – as popular with critics as the box office. This has resulted in not just seven but a staggering **17 Oscars** and millions of dollars for the studio. Telling a story in animated form requires a particularly bizarre kind of personality – an equal mix of childishness and **enormous quantities of patience**. Employees admit that it is a tedious job. They work on something for two years for maybe less than two minutes of film. If you're not a patient kind of person, you just can't take it. And obsessive secrecy characterises the studio's attitude to its future releases, so it is impossible for animators to talk about what they are working on now. What they can tell you, however, is that **it is so difficult to create animated characters which are realistic** that it is pointless even trying. Computer animation's best characters are strictly symbolic representations. This is probably because profound emotions are not always best conveyed by characters who appear to be real creatures.

Strangely enough, for a company that appears to have **discovered some kind of magic formula**, their film *The Incredibles* seems to dispense with everything it has done before. This is because the main characters are all human, rather than animals or other creatures. The film also lasts for two full hours and many shots are slow, or completely still. But **what will surprise viewers most of all is not the story but the message** the film sends out. Every Pixar film has a message and in this film it seems to be that some people are just better than others and their resentful inferiors should just accept the fact that this is the way things are. The Pixar doctrine seems to be that if a story really is good enough, it will reach everybody, not just children – and even **the jokes that younger viewers miss** will somehow enhance their experience of the film. Children live in an adult world and are used to hearing things they don't understand. So part of what makes life interesting is trying to figure things out. So putting things like jokes they don't understand in a movie is fine. Overall, what is special about Pixar is that their appeal is universal. And somehow, it seems that they can do no wrong.

4 Encourage students to consider the importance of getting the right plot, actors, setting and soundtrack. They may find some of the vocabulary on page 132 useful. Ask if they can name the last Oscar winners and whether they think the films should have won or not, giving reasons.

Speaking p135

1 Check students can describe briefly what the situations in the photos show before they match a–e:
1 a snooker match
2 a basketball match/game
3 a Punch and Judy show/children's entertainment
4 an open-air play/theatre performance

Key

All the words refer to people seeing or looking at something.
a photos 1 and 2
b photos 1, 2, 3 and 5
c can refer to someone who sees a crime or other significant event
d refers to someone who doesn't take part in an event but is there to evaluate it in some way
e usually refers to someone watching TV

2 When students have finished the task, check that they know the function of each link word or phrase, and ask them to suggest any others they might need to talk about the pictures. Remind them that the use of linking words will help to make their language more coherent.

Key

well, on the other hand, as for, but, and

Tapescript

Ana: **Well**, these people obviously enjoy going to the theatre. They probably find a live performance much more exciting than watching a play on television. **On the other hand**, the spectators at the basketball match must enjoy supporting their team, together with all the other fans. **As for** the atmosphere in each case – well, it's completely different. At the theatre you must be quiet as a member of the audience. Everyone is concentrating on what the actors are doing. **But** at a basketball match you can stand up **and** feel like you're taking part in the match on the court yourself. That's part of the fun!

3 Monitor students to make sure they are making links between the pictures, and using linking words appropriately.

Use of English p136

1 Remind students to read through the title and the text quickly to form a general idea of the content, before focusing on the missing information.

Key

Classical music is being played at a railway station to drive away young people who have been causing trouble. This has been successful.

2 Remind students that the missing words tend to be short words such as prepositions, pronouns, linking words, etc.

Key

1	of	9	up
2	as	10	away
3	a	11	in/up
4	been	12	only
5	not	13	longer
6	or/like	14	however/but
7	so/and	15	being
8	which/that		

4 Ask students to underline the key words in the first sentence and to make connections with the head word if possible, e.g. b is *forced* > made to do something.

Key

a   no longer able
b   are made to listen to
c   get rid of
d   has slipped his mind

Vocabulary p137

1 Ask students to find a three-part phrasal verb in the text on page 136 (*getting up to* after gap 5) and to say what it means (*doing* – often, and in this case, *something bad or disapproved of*). You could ask students to find the appropriate meaning for each gap from 1–7 before they complete the missing particle.

Key

a	4 out	d	5 up	f	7 up
b	6 out	e	3 on	g	2 away
c	1 up				

2 **Key and suggested answers**
a   more slowly, up
b   out, rude/strange
c   on, pack his bags and leave
d   up, take advantage of you
e   out, cope/bring up the children
f   spoilt/selfish, in

3 Check that students understand the meaning of the phrasal verbs in a–f and ask them to suggest synonyms.

Key and suggested answers

a fell out with – argued with
b came up with – invented
c keep up with – keep pace with
d run out of – don't have any more
e stick up for – defend yourself
f going on at – nagging

Optional activity

Dictate the following questions to students to discuss in pairs or small groups. Ask them to add two or three more questions to ask each other using other phrasal verbs from the task.

1 What do you usually do when you fall out with someone?
2 What things do you find difficult to put up with?
3 Who do you get on best with in your family?

Writing p138

1 Ask students what normally makes them want to see a film, e.g. cinema trailers, TV or radio adverts, media reviews, friends' recommendations. Ask which they think are most reliable as an indication of how good a film is.

2 Once students have decided, ask them to read the model answer and find examples of a–e.

Suggested answers

a, b, e (d is possible depending on the type of film)
The model answer includes all these elements.

3 Remind students of the importance of including all the information they are asked for, and of thinking about the purpose of their writing and the intended audience.

Key

a Yes   b Yes

4 Students can check in a dictionary if they have problems.

Key

a gripping
b ruthless
c callous
d courageous
e superb
f haunting
g mischievous
h bloodthirsty
i seductive
j outstanding

5 Check that students understand all the adjectives and if necessary ask them to suggest synonyms. Point out that they can 'mix and match' the adjectives with different nouns as appropriate, but check that they are using correct collocations.

6 Key

Strong: c, d, f, g, h
Medium: a, e
Weak: b, i

Some of the strong adverbs (*utterly, absolutely, completely,* and *totally*) combine best with adjectives that already imply an extreme: *gripping, action-packed, spine-chilling, spectacular, tremendous, fantastic, amazing, stunning.*
Of the medium adverbs, *really* and *rather* combine with most adjectives, but *rather* can sound odd with adjectives that imply an extreme, e.g. not *rather fantastic.*
The weak adverbs go best with less extreme adjectives, especially those with a negative implication: *slow-moving, predictable, far-fetched, awkward, wooden, uninspired, unconvincing, mediocre, disappointing.*

7 Encourage students to try to include some of the language from exercises 4–6 in their plan.

For an assessed authentic answer to this Writing task, see page 16 of the *Writing and Speaking Assessment Booklet* in the Teacher's Pack.

Review p140

1 Key

b 1 can be heard
c 2 are often hired
d 6 are written
e 7 be found
f 4 is organised
g 5 are always held

2 Key

a onlookers   c witnesses   e audience
b observer   d spectators   f viewers

3 Key

a of/about doing away with
b must have fallen out/have surely fallen out
c of putting up with
d to make up for forgetting
e able to come up with

4 Key

1 thrilling   5 uninspiring
2 gripping   6 wooden
3 spectacular   7 disappointing
4 awkward

A changing world

Lead in p141

1 If students know anything about the environmental situation of the Arctic, get feedback and then ask them to compare what they know with the short extract. Ask if they know of any areas in their own countries which might be under threat in some way and what could be done or is already being done about it.

Suggested answers

a The energy industry would argue that we are running out of oil globally and need to exploit new sources.
Environmentalists would be against it because wildlife and their natural habitats would be threatened or destroyed, for what may provide only a limited source of energy.

2 See if students can add one or two more ideas, e.g. have five-minute showers instead of long baths to save on heating water.

Reading p142

1 Before students do the task, ask them to look at the introduction to the text and the five places named, to see if they already know what environmental problem is associated with each one.

Key

1	Greenland	4	the Sahara Desert
2	the North Atlantic	5	the Amazon Forest
3	the Tibetan Plateau		

2 You might like to do one or two examples as a whole class first. Remind students of this technique on pages 34 and 70, and ask if and how it helped. Brainstorm as many synonymous phrases as students can suggest, perhaps setting a time limit. (The specific references in the text are given in the key to exercise 3.)

3 Key

1 B *flourish of vegetation* (l. 20)
2 E *the entire region lay beneath the sea* (l. 75–76)
3 D *Surface water ... is first cooled* (l. 57–58); *warm water ... moves upward* (l. 61–62)
4 A *collapse of the myriad ecosystems, extinction of species* (l. 6–7)
5 C *all but disappear* (l. 48)
6 B *food available for plankton* (l. 30–31)
7/8 C *frozen wastes ... if the permafrost melts* (l.-50–52)
   E *buried under snow and ice, the region acts as a giant mirror ... to keep a lid on global warming* (l. 81–83)
9 A *the same order of magnitude as from the twentieth century's total fossil fuel output* (l.15–16)
10 D *heavier rains* (l. 67), *temperature could drop 10°C or more* (l. 71)
11 B *crop damage from pests could soar* (l. 40–41)
12 E *fossils of marine animals can be found in mountain ridges* (l. 76–77)

Check the meaning of any unknown vocabulary, particularly those related to the topic, e.g. *biodiverse* (l. 2), *ecosystem* (l. 6), *fossil fuels* (l. 11), *fertile* (l.-22), *equator* (l. 60), *jet streams* (l. 87).

Vocabulary p144

1 When students have finished the task, ask them to give synonyms of each phrase and ask if they have similar expressions in their own language using *earth*, *world* or *ground*, or their equivalents.

Key

a	earth	d	world	g	earth
b	world	e	ground	h	ground
c	ground	f	earth	i	world

2 Suggest students compare answers in small groups to see which sentences best illustrate the meaning of the expressions.

Suggested answers

a ... think it's the best place I've ever eaten.
b ... been working too hard and really needs a rest.
c ... don't try to get any sense out of her!
d ... I'd do everything to protect you.
e ... he took her on a holiday to a beautiful Caribbean island.
f ... told us you'd be back at 10 p.m. and it's gone midnight!

3

> **Optional activity**
> Ask students to find other examples or expressions with *world*, *earth* or *ground* in their dictionaries. Get feedback from the whole class.

Grammar p144

1 Remind students that emphatic statements are most commonly found in formal, and often written language. As they do the exercise, ask them to suggest where they might read sentences a–h.

Key and suggested answers

a had (news report)
b had (personal account of an event)
c will (official report)
d do (scientific report)
e are (notice at airport/on plane)
f should (security notice at airport)
g can (written account)
h did (news report)

2 Ensure students think carefully about the tense and which auxiliary verb goes with the main verb in each sentence.

Key

a Scarcely had the band announced their world tour when they were forced to cancel it.
b Not only is the planet becoming polluted but it is getting warmer too.
c In no way was the lorry driver to blame for the crash.
d No sooner had the prince arrived in the ski resort than he was besieged by reporters.
e Little can Shakespeare's contemporaries have guessed how enduring his plays would prove to be.

f Nowhere in the world do they serve such delicious food as in Italy!
g Not until a few years ago did anyone know about the existence of the buried treasure.
h Only by chance did botanists discover the rare plant growing under a rock.

3 Before students do the exercise refer them to *Inversion* point 2 on page 181 of the Grammar Reference, as they will need to use some of the expressions beginning with *only* and *no*. Students may have more than one answer, so you could ask them to compare answers in pairs or groups.

Suggested answers

a No sooner had we driven off to the coast than we got a puncture.
b Nowhere in the house could I find a pencil.
c Little did she know what lay in store for her when she went to work that day.
d Only by luck were we passing by as the boy fell down the cliff.
e In no way was the mistake your fault.
f Not only is this flat damp, it's draughty as well.
g Only recently did we find out his true identity.
h No sooner had they got to the summit than a thick fog descended.

4 If students can't think of ideas from recent news stories, suggest they talk about ideas related to their own personal experience, e.g. *It came as something of a shock when I first left home and lived on my own.*

5 Refer students to the section on *Emphatic structures with it and what* on page 182 of the Grammar Reference before they do the task.

Key

a What I'm curious to know is who you went to the disco with last night.
b Mowing the lawn is the job I hate most when gardening.
c What I've suggested is that John and Clare wait for another year before they get married./What I've suggested to John and Clare is that they wait for another year before they get married.
d All I'm worried about is how much a cruise would cost/the cost of a cruise.
e The thing you didn't tell me about English was that the grammar would be so hard.
f The person who upset your mother was you, not me.

g My reason for leaving work early today is that I'm holding a dinner party for twenty people tonight.

h The only place you'll get a gorilla suit for the fancy-dress tomorrow is in a joke shop.

Listening p146

1 Ask students to name other forms of alternative energy as well as wind-powered energy, e.g. solar energy, tidal power, hydro-electric. Find out if alternative energy sources are becoming more popular in their countries.

Suggested answers

1 Gas- or coal-fired power stations are relatively safe, but they use valuable fossil fuels and are ugly for local residents.

2 Wind turbines are renewable, safe and cheap, but can spoil the natural beauty of the countryside.

3 Oil can be dangerous to extract, especially at sea, and is becoming more expensive as resources run out. It severely pollutes the sea and damages marine life if there is an oil spillage.

4 Hydroelectric power is clean and safe, but dams are expensive to build and local communities may need to be relocated.

2 Ask students if the speakers mentioned any other advantages or disadvantages they didn't think of. (The tapescript here with highlighted answers also applies to exercise 3.)

Tapescript

Speaker 1

It's common knowledge that the world's oil and gas supplies aren't inexhaustible. **So I was prepared to accept the fact** that this nuclear power station needed to be built and this was as good a place as any to site it. It doesn't particularly worry me that this source of energy's expensive to produce – let's face it, we just have to put up with that. What is much more problematic is how to get rid of the by-product. **It can remain highly toxic for years, and, as we know to our cost, accidents can devastate huge areas**. Once we crack the problem of disposing of that, I think there'll be less opposition to the use of nuclear power.

Speaker 2

At first, I was dead against the whole idea. I thought anyone who supported anything to do with nuclear power wasn't worth giving the time of day to. The ironic thing is that, from what I've heard on the news recently, it seems this kind of energy turns out to be something that can have less harmful effects on the environment than we thought, which is a bit of an eye-opener, to tell the truth! But I suppose that one of the reservations **I still have about it is that there are so many other energy sources that remain untapped as yet. So I say – let's go for those.**

Speaker 3

I started out thinking that this anti-nuclear power movement was a lot of fuss about nothing. As far as I was concerned, as long as I had heating and lighting, **I didn't care a hoot about how it reached me.** I was far too busy with the nitty-gritty of getting through the week, if you understand me. But when it's a question of 'in your own back yard', you start to ask yourself a few questions about what right we have to interfere with this beautiful world we live in. **Maybe we should stop now before we destroy it completely.** But let's face it, what difference does it make what I think?

Speaker 4

I knew, which I'm sure a lot of people don't, that **nuclear power plants emit virtually no greenhouse gases**. Apparently, if all the existing nuclear power plants were shut down and replaced with equally powerful energy from non-nuclear sources, there would be a huge increase in the amount of pollution in the atmosphere. It's a sobering thought and a powerful argument for nuclear power, isn't it? But living down the road from a nuclear power station, or any other kind of power station is another matter. Ultimately, **it makes the area an undesirable location for residents.**

Speaker 5

I must admit that in the beginning **I was pretty ignorant about what using nuclear power really meant**. I thought it might create employment in the area but that's about all. But from what I've read since, it seems that one of the biggest objections to the siting of nuclear power stations is that the local people aren't consulted. In our case, nothing could have been further from the truth. Everyone got sent a letter outlining the proposal, and there were countless follow-up meetings – where, incidentally, usually only a handful of people turned up! But the point is that, however open people are about what nuclear power means, in the long run **there's still that unknown quantity in terms of what effect it might have.**

3 Students may already be able to answer some of the questions having listened to the recording for exercise 2, but play the recording twice again if necessary (the tapescript with highlighted answers is with exercise 2 above).

Key

1 D   2 H   3 F   4 B   C   6 H   7 G   8 E   9 B
10 F

4 Ask students how they personally could protest and how larger organisations e.g. Greenpeace, organise protests. Ask them to consider how effective these actions might be. You could broaden the discussion to whether it is ever right to break the law in order to make a protest, and what positive or negative effects such actions might have.

Suggested answers

Writing letters to politicians/newspapers, joining a politically active group, signing petitions, taking part in demonstrations, refusing to buy certain products or boycotting particular firms, etc.

Speaking p147

1 Elicit the correct vocabulary to refer to each photo (1 *museum* or *art gallery*, 2 *shopping mall*, 3 *funfair* or *amusement park*, 4 *skateboard park*). Divide students into small groups to think of three more suggestions and then take a class vote on the best ones.

2 The photos show: (5) *a wildlife meadow/area* (6) *apartment blocks/flats* (7) *outdoor café/ restaurant*.

3 Check that students understand the verbs in a–h and are using them with appropriate phrases in 1–8. Point out that there are various possible combinations.

Suggested answers

a	4, 5	e	4
b	4, 6, 8	f	2, 4
c	4, 6, 7, 8	g	1
d	2, 3, 4	h	6, 8

4 Ask students to suggest some 'do's and don'ts' for Part 3 before they do the task. Refer them to the advice in previous Speaking sections if necessary. They can then compare their ideas with what the candidates do well or badly.

Suggested answers

They begin straight away so they don't waste valuable time. The girl forgets what the task is, giving the impression that she hasn't been concentrating. The boy asks how much time they have left, which interrupts the discussion. Otherwise they make a good attempt at the task and interact well.

Tapescript

Examiner:	Imagine that there is a large disused area of land in your town. Here are some ideas for redeveloping it. Talk to each other about the benefits and drawbacks of these ideas for redeveloping the disused area of land, then decide which two would be in the best interests of the town's inhabitants.
Male:	So, shall we start with the blocks of flats?
Female:	Why not? Er ... sorry, I've forgotten what you asked us to do.
Examiner:	Talk to each other about the benefits and drawbacks of these ideas for redeveloping the disused area of land, then decide which two would be in the best interests of the town's inhabitants.
Female:	Oh, yes. Well, the idea of providing housing would certainly appeal to most people, although I'm not sure if everyone would want to live in flats like these.
Male:	Yes, I see what you mean. The housing would certainly be needed if the area is being redeveloped, so the flats might be very welcome – but maybe people would like something more attractive in the area as well ...
Female:	Yes, and also by building even more flats, you increase the numbers of people living in the area – and there'll be more cars and more congestion, so more housing may not be in the best interests of the inhabitants.
Male:	Good point. Actually, in my opinion, the skateboard park might be an idea worth considering. It would certainly encourage people to come and enjoy themselves – and everyone seems to be interested in sport, don't you think?
Female:	Well, most people are, I suppose. And that would definitely be one reason for choosing the skateboard park. But let's think about the others before we make a decision, shall we?

Male:	Of course. What about this one – a theme park – that would be something completely different, wouldn't it? It would be great for young people, and the rest of the community!
Female:	I'm afraid I don't really agree with you at all. Theme parks are noisy, and they don't really appeal to everybody. Maybe the idea of a museum and art gallery would appeal to more people and be more useful for the community as a whole – for schools, you know, educational visits, and so on.
Male:	Actually, I don't think the museum or art gallery would be as much fun as a theme park! Er … have we still got more time?

5 Monitor pairs to make sure they are talking about all the options before making a decision and encourage them to use the language in the *Suggesting alternatives* box where possible. Give a time limit of four minutes. As an extension to the task, you could ask students to talk about ways their own town or neighbourhood could be improved.

Use of English p148

1 Key

They are all made from recycled materials, e.g. the 'robot' is made from an old lawnmower and the top of an oven, the fish are made from car parts, the elephant is made from old TV sets, the model of the Taj Mahal is made of tin, and the 'mosaic' is made from bottles and pieces of tile.

2 Remind students of the importance of reading through the text first to get a general idea and to pay attention to parts of speech before and after the missing word.

Key

1 C   2 D   3 C   4 A   5 D   6 B   7 C   8 A   9 D   10 B   11 B   12 B

3 Refer students back to the text to see the use and context of the missing words.

Key

a   lead
b   main

c   amount
d   waste

Vocabulary p149

1 Key

b i   c f   d h   e g

2 Key

a   e, g
b   e, g
c   c, f

d   b, i
e   c, f
f   d, h

Writing p150

2 Before students read the memo and notes, ask them to think of any problems a large company (or their school or college) might have with recycling and waste, and if they can think of any simple or practical solutions for these. Students could then compare their ideas with the input text. Point out that the aim of this task is to make them read the information carefully so that they are clear what they are writing, to whom and with what purpose.

Key

1   managing director
2   memo

3   proposal

3 Key

a   ✓
b   too informal
c   ✓
d   ✓
e   ✓

f   too informal
g   too informal
h   ✓
i   too informal
j   too informal

4 As students to re-read and underline or note the key points in the memo and notes in 2, before reading the *How to do it* box on page 151.

Key

a   separate sections with headings
b   Yes
c   Yes

5 Remind students of the importance of rephrasing information to meet the word limit. Using the gerund as the subject of a sentence, or passive forms can reduce sentence length.

Suggested answers

a Encouraging staff to use the recycling bins could reduce waste.
b Posters could be used to remind staff to be more energy-conscious.
c Solar panels installed in the roof would reduce our bills.

6 The purpose of this task is to remind students of the importance of editing their work. They could practise this by checking each other's work and suggesting improvements.

For an assessed authentic answer to this Writing task, see page 17 of the *Writing and Speaking Assessment Booklet* in the Teacher's Pack.

Review p152

1 Key

a	ground	e	world	i	world
b	earth	f	ground	j	world
c	world	g	earth	k	earth
d	ground	h	world	l	world

2 Key

a	provide (2)	e	encourage (8)
b	promote (5)	f	was created (6)
c	caused (1)	g	worsened (4)
d	generated (7)	h	cater for (2)

3 Key

a reduction
b varies
c environmental

4 Key

a increasingly, progressively
c irregularly, occasionally
d rarely, infrequently
e annually, yearly
f presently, currently

5 Suggested answers

a People should be persuaded to recycle unwanted objects such as mobile phones.
b Creating parks would make the area more pleasant for residents.

Unit and Progress Tests

Unit 1 Test

1 Decide which of character adjectives 1–10 best describe the person required for each job a–j.

a Older person required to take on responsible administrative position. ....

b We are looking for a hard-working young person who is ready to work long hours and do the job thoroughly. ....

c Do you enjoy working alone and making your own decisions? Then this is the job for you! ....

d No experience or qualifications needed. We just want you to be as excited about outdoor pursuits as the kids you will be working with! ....

e High salary and excellent promotion prospects for a real high-flyer who is looking to go far. ....

f Our company seeks someone who can make hard choices, lead a team, and stand by their opinions. ....

g Clear-thinking mathematician required. ....

h If you can talk to people in difficult situations, talk to us about a career in counselling. ....

i Can you put the needs of others before your own? ....

j Are you curious about the world around you? Do you want to know the answers to all sorts of problems? Start by finding out more about a career with us. ....

1	independent
2	mature
3	caring
4	inquisitive
5	decisive
6	conscientious
7	ambitious
8	logical
9	enthusiastic
10	tactful

(10 marks)

2 Circle the adjective which best describes the people in 1–5.

1 a lottery winner
  a careless   b lucky   c sensitive

2 a marriage guidance counsellor
  a thick-skinned   b outgoing   c tactful

3 a likeable, trustworthy guy
  a real   b genuine   c realistic

4 a liar
  a unmotivated   b uninterested   c dishonest

5 a baby
  a careless   b helpless   c thoughtful

(5 marks)

3 Circle the odd word out in each group a–e.

a logical	practical	vague	rational
b thoughtful	sensible	considerate	helpful
c genuine	honest	truthful	thick-skinned
d creative	imaginative	inquisitive	conscientious
e dishonest	unreliable	introvert	trustworthy

(5 marks)

4 Jenny has written a poem about her boyfriends. Complete 1–5 with the correct character adjectives.

The boys I love

I love my Bert
He's such an e.................... (1)
He likes to be the centre of attention!

And I love Paul
He's very t.................... (2)
He always buys flowers on my birthday!

And then there's Nigel
He's very l.................... (3)
Always finds answers to my problems!

And the lovely Patrick
Who's very e.................. (4)
Gets very excited about everything!

And finally Cliff
Who's very i....................... (5)
And is always asking questions about my boyfriends!!

(5 marks)

5 Tom is in charge of the tombola at the village fete. Circle the correct word to complete each phrase a–e, then complete gaps 1–5 in the dialogue with a–e.

a *starter's/beginner's* luck
b don't *push/pull* your luck
c I'm afraid you're *outside/out* of luck.

d the luck of the *pick/draw*
e by a *stroke/blow* of luck

(5 marks)

Customer: How do I play?
Tom: Put your hand in the box and choose a ticket. If, (1) .... you choose a good ticket, you win. If not, you lose. It's all about being lucky. It's (2) .... – literally!
Customer: Here goes. Ah, number 101. Is that any good?
Tom: Yes. You've won the second prize. A bike.
Customer: It must be (3) .... I've never played this game before. Can I buy another ten tickets?
Tom: Yes. But (4) .... This time you probably won't win.
Customer: OK. I'll just buy one. Number 66. Does that win?
Tom: No. (5) .... You haven't won.
Customer: Oh, hang on. It's upside down. 99. Does that win?
Tom: Yes, you've won a holiday! You're very lucky, aren't you?

(5 marks)

6 Circle the correct prepositions in 1–5 to complete this character reference.

I am writing (1) *on/at/in* behalf of Tim Smith, who has applied to be a group leader at your youth centre. Tim gets (2) *at/in/on* well with young people and is used (3) *for/at/to* organising sports and other activities. Moreover, when it comes (4) *for/at/to* making decisions, he is very decisive. I therefore have no hesitation (5) *in/on/at* recommending Tim.

(5 marks)

7 Decide which tenses are shown in bold in 1–5 below.

1 **She'll be preparing** for the exam all next week.   ....
2 I **was walking** into town when I saw them at the restaurant.   ....
3 The film **had already started** by the time we got there.   ....
4 My **sister's been learning** Spanish since her trip there last year.   ....
5 **We're always trying** to work hard and please our teacher.   ....

(10 marks)

Total: /50

Unit 2 Test

1 Match words a–e with the words or phrases they collocate with (1–5).

a bitterly   ....
b meet   ....
c absolutely   ....
d deeply   ....
e break   ....

1 grateful
2 your word
3 disappointed
4 amazed
5 with your approval

(5 marks)

2 Complete sentences a–e with the collocations in exercise 1 and other words where necessary.

a 'I've been training for years for the Olympics, and, now, a week before it starts, I've broken my arm!'
'You must ....'

b 'I can't tell you how much I appreciate all your help. I ....
....'

c 'You must ....
when you realised you'd got the winning lottery numbers!'

d 'If the new furniture I've ordered .... ,
.... we can always change it.'

e 'You shouldn't make a promise if you think you might ....
....'

(10 marks)

3 Complete a–e with nouns and adjectives formed from the word in italics in each sentence.

a I'll never *forget* my trip to Mexico. It was absolutely ....

b When the managing director *revealed* that the head of sales had been committing fraud for years it came as a shocking ....

c A single piece of wood was used to *carve* this beautiful horse's head. I'm sure you'll agree it's a wonderful ....

d It *amazes* me that my younger brother is a successful pop star. Whenever I see him on TV I'm filled with ....

e Our school doesn't *require* students to wear a uniform. It isn't one of the ....

(10 marks)

4 Complete the gaps in the text about motor racing with 10 of words a–o.

a warmly	e memorable	i from	m swept
b passionately	f to	j memory	n put
c fiercely	g into	k draws	o pulls
d earn	h within	l set	

I've always been (1) ………….. interested in motor racing. I know it's not
(2) ………….. everybody's taste, and recently its interest as a spectator sport
has been seriously called (3) …………. question. However, most of my friends
were (4) ………….. jealous when I told them I was going to Monza in Italy to
see a race. To some people, motor racing is one of the main (5) ………….. of
Italy. It turned out to be one of the most (6) ………….. occasions in my life.
Let me (7) ………….. the scene. As you enter the circuit, you are (8) …………..
up by the noise of the cars and by the huge crowds. Frankly, if you've never
stood (9) ………….. earshot of a Formula 1 car, you've heard nothing! Then
the race starts, and the speeds are fantastic. And what a way to
(10) ……………… a living!

(20 marks)

5 Match a–e with statements 1–5 below.
   a parade   ……….
   b contribution   ……….
   c festival   ……….
   d souvenir   ……….
   e tradition   ……….

1 'Every Christmas we buy a tree and decorate it.'
2 'That's a mask I bought in Peru – it reminds me of my trip.'
3 'It was great! We walked down Bourbon Street in new Orleans during Mardi
   Gras, following a band.'
4 'We've been going every year since it started. It's two days' worth of great music
   and entertainment.'
5 'Here's some money for the charity collection.'

(5 marks)

Total: /50

Unit 3 Test

1 Circle the phrase, a or b, which is closest in meaning to the phrases in italics in each of 1–5.

1 Unfortunately, *it seems highly probable* that the trip will be cancelled.
   a it's on the cards   b there's no way

2 Jake *was very upset* when he heard about the accident.
   a broke down   b broke up

3 It was a great show. Thank you very much everybody. You all *worked extremely hard*.
   a gave it everything you had   b lacked talent

4 Now that I'm fifty, I don't enjoy doing all the adventurous things I did when I was a young man. I'm *getting old*.
   a getting to the top   b not getting any younger

5 Don't worry about your promotion. *It will happen soon*.
   a It's in the pipeline.   b It's in the long run.

(10 marks)

2 Complete each of sentences a–e with an expression that includes the words in brackets.

a My great-grandfather is ninety-five, in other words he's .... (hills)
b Jo is very mature for her age. She's got .... (shoulders)
c Phil is very ambitious. He wants to .... (mark)
d At the moment, there are no signs of improvement, but hopefully, things will get better .... (run)
e Although he's 50 now, my uncle Frank is going snowboarding next week. He's still .... (heart)

(10 marks)

3 Circle the correct word in italics for each of 1–10 to complete the text about reality TV.

> The public simply can't get enough of reality 'search for a star' shows, and just about every TV company in the world has either come up *to/with* (1) their own version of such a show, or has one *in/on* (2) the pipeline. Last weekend, thousands of people turned *up/down* (3) for auditions of New Pop Star. All sorts of people were there, all of them ready to *do/make* (4) the sacrifices needed to *break/beat* (5) the competition and *get/make* (6) it to the top. There were toddlers, teenagers and some people who were old enough to know *bigger/better* (7). As they queued to perform, few of the wannabes knew exactly what lay *in/on* (8) store for them. The outcome for the majority of them, however, was being humiliatingly put *up/down* (9) by a panel of 'experts' and rejected for *lacking/wanting* (10) the talent to be a star.

(10 marks)

4 Read the text about Jennifer and circle five true statements from a–h below.

> Jennifer had felt for a long time that she wasn't getting any younger, and that she should do something to get fit. She'd never liked sport much, especially team sports, so she decided to join an aerobics class. Everybody else there was younger than her, which made her feel really old. Nobody else, however, seemed to notice that she was well over thirty. In her first class, Jennifer was hopeless, and couldn't keep up. Her instructor criticised her and made Jennifer cry. Even her best friend laughed at her, and the two of them had a terrible argument. So, Jennifer decided to change her lifestyle, cutting out fast food and alcohol, and now she goes to aerobics all the time and really works hard.

a She broke down.
b She felt her age.
c She looked her age.
d She made sacrifices.
e She was put down.
f Her friend put her up.
g She broke up an argument.
h She puts her heart and soul into aerobics.

(10 marks)

5 Read about the five people who have played a role in Claire's life, then answer questions a–e.

Jake brought her up.
Paul turned her down.
Kate put her up.
Carl turned up.
Mark broke down.

a Who let her stay when she didn't have anywhere to live?

....

b Who arrived unexpectedly?

....

c Who was her father and looked after her when she was a child?

....

d Who rejected her?

....

e Who started crying when she said she couldn't marry him?

....

(10 marks)

Total: /50

Unit 4 Test

1 Circle one word in each group a–f that does not belong to the animal.

a	eagle:	beak	tusk	claw
b	fish:	horn	scale	fin
c	dolphin:	fin	flipper	mane
d	bee:	antenna	wing	beak
e	bull:	paw	hoof	horn
f	lion:	mane	shell	claw

(12 marks)

2 Read the office gossip about Jane, Pete and Edward, then answer questions a–g below.

'Well, Jane is getting married at the weekend, so she was celebrating with all her friends last night. Apparently, she had a fantastic night out. But of course she hasn't done any of her work, so she'll be in trouble with her boss. And Pete had to make a speech at the Women's Institute last night. He was very nervous and could hardly eat beforehand. And of course he was the only man and the only person under 50 there! At least his speech was good, unlike Edward's. Not only did he make a real mess of his speech at last week's conference, he also revealed secret information about one of our new products, so he's not at all popular at the moment!'

a Who let the cat out of the bag?   ....
b Who had a whale of a time?   ....
c Who was a fish out of water?   ....
d Who had a hen party?   ....
e Who made a dog's dinner of things?   ....
f Who had butterflies?   ....
g Which two people are in the doghouse?   ....

(16 marks)

3 Complete the missing prepositions in sentences a–g.

a Some people think that a meteor may one day wipe .... life on earth.

b According .... financial experts the economy is improving.

c Marco Polo journeyed .... miles to reach China.

d Apparently the motorway pile-up started when a car collided .... a van.

e Why don't you finish .... the last piece of cake – there's only a small bit left.

f Sit down and make yourself .... home and I'll be right with you.

g Prices have been increasing .... such a rate that I can't make ends meet.

(14 marks)

4 Decide which of a–c completes the phrases in sentences 1–4.

1 Frank did all the .... work. Penny just made the tea!
a dog   b horse   c donkey

2 I can't believe my last boyfriend turned out to be such a .... in the grass.
a rabbit   b cat   c snake

3 Gary rarely leaves anything on his plate; he eats like a ....
a donkey   b horse   c bull

4 Danny .... on about his new car, but I wasn't listening.
a rabbited   b bulled   c butterflied

(8 marks)

Total: /50

Unit 5 Test

1 Number the parts of the body a–j from 1–10, working from the top downwards.

a cheek   ....
b chin   ....
c waist   ....
d shin   ....
e rib   ....
f shoulder ....
g thigh   ....
h ankle   ....
i hip   ....
j heel   ....

(10 marks)

2 Circle the correct answers to questions a–e.

a Which goes red when you're embarrassed?   chin   cheek
b Which protect your lungs?   ribs   shins
c Which is on the end of your arm?   wrist   ankle
d Which is part of your leg?   shin   chin
e Which do you put a belt round?   thigh   waist

(10 marks)

3 Match a–e with 1–5 to form collocations connected with health.

a high   ....   1 shoulder
b fractured   ....   2 temperature
c searing   ....   3 pain
d tooth   ....   4 skull
e dislocated ....   5 ache

(5 marks)

4 Decide which of the collocations from exercise 3 the medical experts are referring to in a–e.

a 'OK. It's just popped out. This may hurt a little. There we are. Good as new.' ....

b 'So, you say it really hurts, and it's like a sudden, burning sensation.' ....

c 'There's lots of decay here. We'll have to drill it out and put in a filling.' ....

d 'Well, according to my thermometer you have a fever!' ....

e 'That bang on the head was more serious than I thought. We'll have to get you to hospital.' ....

(5 marks)

5 Complete book titles a–j with a word made from the word in italics in the 'blurb' below each one.

a .... of the fittest

Best-selling book about how animals fight to *survive* in Africa.

b .... WEATHER

An amazing true story about how three friends had to *tolerate* the extreme heat of the day and freezing cold of night while crossing a desert on foot.

c .... **BEHAVIOUR**

A disturbing account of life among football fans. Travel with them as they fight other fans and *threaten* ordinary people.

d **Big Book of** .... **Breakthroughs**

A comprehensive history of the greatest inventions and discoveries in *technology* during the last two hundred years.

e **THE** .... **WAR**

Military expert James Good argues that major countries didn't do everything they could to *avoid* the war and that it shouldn't have happened.

f HOW TO BE A CAR ....

The book that tells the *mechanically* minded everything they need to know to get into this rewarding job.

g **An** .... **level of POLLUTION**?

In this ground-breaking book, ecologists ask how much pollution we can *accept* in the world. Some of their conclusions are fascinating.

h **An** .... **for everything**

An entertaining book in which top scientists from around the world try to *explain* some of science's most complex puzzles in simple terms.

i MY TOP TEN .... FOR NEXT YEAR

Astrologer Jan Perkins *predicts* pop star break ups and celebrity surprises in the coming year.

j *A* .... *holiday*

A new novel by Lesley Wilde in which an elderly woman shares her *memories* of a summer forty years ago which changed her life.

(20 marks)

Total: /50

Unit 6 Test

1 Read the information in a–e about how five friends got home from a restaurant, and complete the gaps with the correct form of 1–5.

1	stagger	a	Patrick hit his leg on the table as he stood up. He .... home.
2	limp	b	Sam was very tired and walked slowly with heavy steps. He .... home.
3	hobble	c	Peter didn't want to wake his wife when he got in. He .... indoors.
4	creep	d	Paul has an old and very painful foot injury. He .... home.
5	plod	e	Frank didn't feel very well and was unsteady on his feet. He .... home.

(5 marks)

2 Match a–j with 1–10 below to form complete phrases.

a	sooner or	....	1	away
b	ring	....	2	right
c	under	....	3	a sudden
d	more or	....	4	later
e	right	....	5	less
f	more than	....	6	rights
g	before	....	7	true
h	in the	....	8	likely
i	all of	....	9	false pretences
j	by	....	10	long

(5 marks)

3 Find and correct the one wrong word in each sentence a–h.

a If only all our dreams would get true. ....

b We got to know each other little by less. ....

c Jackie is useless at sport. She has two false feet. ....

d Becky is absolutely committed of her studies. ....

e Wait a moment. I'll be right off. ....

f Installing the alarm gave us a false mood of security. We still got burgled! ....

g She's very self-conscious with her appearance. ....

h Joe may be poor, but on the other foot, he seems very happy. ....

(16 marks)

4 For each of a–h, rewrite the part of the sentence in italics using phrases from exercise 2.

a He told me he was an astronaut, but *I don't believe it.*
It doesn't ....

b I'm sure she'll pass. It's *highly probable.*
It's ....

c Personally, I think Jake *has justice on his side.* Penny started the argument.
Jake is ....

d Don't worry. Margaret will get here *eventually.*
She'll be here ....

e Amazingly, Stubbs got a job as a doctor and diagnosed patients *dishonestly, without any qualifications.*
Stubbs got the job ....

f That's *approximately* right.
That's .... right.

g We'll be on holiday in Jamaica *soon!*
We'll be on holiday ....

h I'll phone her *immediately.*
I'll phone her ....

(16 marks)

5 Choose the correct answer, a or b, to each of questions 1–4.

1 What are leftovers?
a the remains of food from yesterday
b food you bought this morning

2 What is a false economy?
a buying something cheap which isn't worth the money
b buying something very expensive then selling it for more money

3 Where would you find a left-luggage office?
a in a railway station
b in a factory

4 What is a false impression?
a a clear idea of what something is
b an idea which is misleading

(8 marks)

Total: /50

Unit 7 Test

1   Each sentence a–j has a missing preposition or particle, and a missing prefix. Rewrite the relevant parts of the sentence to include them.

   a   He's far too inexperienced and self-centred, and would be completely suitable for a job in which he had to be responsible so many people.
   ....

   b   Peters was sent to prison for driving at over 100 miles an hour – an act that was not only legal but resulted a terrible car crash.
   ....

   c   We all got into the car and set for the national airport – we were going to fly all the way to Australia.
   ....

   d   My brother's hopeless – so decisive. He can never make his mind up, and is always putting decisions.
   ....

   e   I thought the test was very important, but I had been informed. It had no effect my final results at all.
   ....

   f   Allowing children to tell lies and be generally honest can lead more serious behavioural problems later.
   ....

   g   Can you turn the oven? I'm worried that the meat may be cooked – there's nothing worse than dry, burnt meat!
   ....

   h   The only thing that matters is that we discover the source these stories; whether they're true or not is completely relevant.
   ....

   i   Some aspects of philosophy seem contrary to common sense, and at times logical, but don't be put! It's a fascinating subject once you begin to understand it.
   ....

   j   James may seem helpless, but in fact he's incredibly dependent, and will never give until he has achieved his aims.
   ....

(20 marks)

2   Replace the words in italics in a–f using phrasal verbs with *in* or *off*.

   a   We were completely *fooled* by his disguise.
   ....

   b   Terrorists have *exploded* a bomb in the city centre.
   ....

   c   We'd better *postpone* the meeting until Frances feels better.
   ....

d To be honest, what *made* me *dislike* him was his self-centredness.

....

e The soldiers refused to *surrender* even though they were surrounded.

....

f Your most direct route is to *leave* the main road just after you pass the petrol station.

....

(6 marks)

3 Use the word in italics in a–g to form another word that completes the second sentence.

a I really can't see the *benefits* of working so many hours.
I can't see how working so many hours is ....

b Kim's work is *accurate* but not very imaginative.
Although not very imaginative, Kim's work shows a good level of

....

c It was *evident* that Smith was guilty of the crime.
Smith's guilt was proved by the ....

d The star's behaviour showed a disgraceful lack of *morality*.
The star's behaviour was disgracefully ....

e Nelson Mandela's life has *inspired* many people.
For many people, Nelson Mandela's life has been ....

f There was real *drama* in yesterday's events at court.
Yesterday's events at court were really ....

g Children become much more aware as they grow up.
As children grow up they show much more ....

(14 marks)

4 Find and correct five mistakes with word formation in this text about a hurricane.

Hurricane Katrina

One of the most significance hurricanes of recent times was 'Katrina' which was responsible for battering the coast of Louisiana in the USA in September 2005, causing untold devastating. Local authorities were not prepared as they had overestimated the strength of the hurricane. The force of the storm resulted in a number of breaches in the protection system of New Orleans, which in turn led to flooding so catastrophe and extensive that it will take years for the city to recover. Emergency services worked tirelessly during the storm, refusing to give in, but they were capable of stopping the flooding.

1 ....
2 ....
3 ....
4 ....
5 ....

(10 marks)

Total: /50

Unit 8 Test

1 Match a–h to the sets of words (1–8) that could be used to talk about them.

a	tornado	....
b	earthquake	....
c	volcano	....
d	famine	....
e	flood	....
f	drought	....
g	landslide	....
h	contagious disease	....

1	shake	collapse	tremor
2	starve	hunger	food
3	parched	thirst	dry
4	wind	funnel	destruction
5	lava	erupt	active
6	erosion	rocks	fall
7	spread	catch	virus
8	pour	rising	drown

(16 marks)

2 For a–h circle the correct words from the choice in italics.

a Dormant for centuries, Pinatubo erupted *into/out of* the blue and left thousands of people homeless.

b Since the crops were devoured by insects, starvation has haunted this part of Africa, and there is no end *in/at* sight.

c Bear *at/in* mind that the tornado is travelling at over 100 miles an hour, destroying everything in its path!

d *In/On* the long run, deforestation and soil erosion on the upper slopes will lead to rocks crashing down the hillsides and causing enormous damage.

e There has been no rain for months and thousands of lives are *at/for* stake.

f Rising waters have breached the dam, and matters are now *out of/off* our control.

g Every vaccine against disease has some risk, so it's up *for/to* you whether you have it or not.

h Many buildings have collapsed and the roads round here have been torn up – one car I saw was turned *at/on* end, trapping the driver inside.

(16 marks)

3 Use phrases a–h below to complete this film review.

> The film *Touching the Void* tells the story of how Joe Simpson, a mountain climber, falls and breaks his leg in the Andes, and (1) .... hanging from a rope in a crevasse. With Joe (2) .... , his climbing partner faces a tough decision, but in the freezing temperatures and with no food, his own life is (3) .... He (4) .... his mind to cut the rope, leaving Joe for dead. Joe, however, starts to crawl down the mountain, even though there appears to be no (5) .... to this impossible journey. It takes days, without water or painkillers, but (6) .... , he manages to reach base camp and safety. (7) .... of the film, I suppose the moral is that it is (8) .... whether you choose to accept or resist your fate.

a   in the end
b   at the end
c   ends up
d   up to you
e   at stake
f   end in sight
g   out of reach
h   makes up

(8 marks)

4 Circle the correct word in italics to complete each sentence a–j.

a   Eating meat is against my *principles/principals*.
b   The president had to decide whether to declare war or not – she knew it was a *momentary/momentous* decision.
c   This is only a short-*term/-stay* solution to the problem and we can expect further, more drastic measures.
d   I don't like working in a café but I need the money to go to college – it is just a *reason/means* to an end really.
e   I'd say I'm a spontaneous person – I tend to act on the *point/spur* of the moment.
f   Introducing parking fines was a very *critical/controversial* decision – many people objected to it.
g   Before deciding to do voluntary service overseas there are lots of different factors that you need to *measure/weigh* up.
h   If you're at a *short/loose* end this weekend, come over to our place. We're having a barbecue.
i   *Antisocial/Unsocial* behaviour such as vandalism is a major problem in some cities.
j   The resources of many *depopulated/overpopulated* countries in the developing world are severely stretched.

(10 marks)

Total: /50

Unit 9 Test

1 Match crimes a–j with newspaper extracts 1–10.

a	arson	....	1 ... managed to break in to the property by forcing an upstairs window ...
b	murder	....	2 ... experts verified that the painting was not genuine ...
c	fraud	....	3 ... thousands of pounds of damage were caused in the recent factory fire ...
d	burglary	....	4 ... the politician was hit in the face by an angry protester ...
e	assault	....	5 ... was stolen from the back seat of his car which ...
f	forgery	....	6 ... he had literally stolen the identity of the other man in order to gain access to
g	theft	....	his finances ...
h	blackmail	....	7 ... armed with shotguns forced their way into the bank ...
i	robbery	....	8 ... threatened to send the photos to the national press if she did not pay ...
j	mugging	....	9 ... was walking home when a man wielding a knife forced him to hand over ....
			10 ... police are treating the death of the eminent scientist as suspicious ...

(10 marks)

2 Put events a–g in order from what happened to the criminal first (1) to what happened last (7).

a He appealed against the sentence. ....
b He was taken into custody.   ....
c He was released on parole.   ....
d He was charged with an offence. ....
e He committed a crime.   ....
f He was sentenced to prison.   ....
g He was arrested by the police.   ....

(14 marks)

3 Circle the phrase (a or b) which correctly completes each sentence 1–5.

1 If you hold out .... , I'll give you something nice!
  a your hand   b your eyes

2 We are interested in checking out ....
  a the papers to the students   b the facilities at the gym

3 It was such a .... that she still hasn't got over it.
  a nasty shock   b good job

4 I can't work out ....
  a how much those groceries cost   b for such an unpleasant boss

5 The children didn't set out .... for school today and got in trouble.
  a their homework   b early enough

(5 marks)

4 Replace phrases 1–8 in the judge's speech with the phrase with the most similar meaning from a–h.

> 'John Blagger, you are (1) *accused of* assault and causing wilful damage to property. The (2) *effect of* your behaviour towards your victims has in some cases been very serious, and many of them have found it difficult to (3) *recover from* their ordeal. You are also (4) *at fault* for the damage caused, although it has been difficult to (5) *calculate* the exact cost of this. (6) *In conclusion*, therefore, I sentence you to 50 hours of community service. You may not (7) *ask the court to change its decision as regards* this sentence. (8) *Taking everything into consideration*, I think this is the best solution for everybody.'

a   to blame
b   appeal against
c   to sum up
d   charged with
e   on balance
f   result of
g   get over
h   work out

(16 marks)

5 Decide which preposition can be used to complete each of the three sentences in a–e.

a   I can't work .... the answer to this mathematical problem.
My favourite singer has just brought .... a new album.
Could you put .... the lights, please?

b   There is a lot of scope .... improvement in the health service.
William was given over a million pounds as compensation .... the injuries he received in the accident.
Jenkins was arrested .... assault.

c   I wonder what your view .... the situation is?
Both men were eventually found guilty .... fraud.
The best way .... observing wildlife is to stay very still and wear camouflage.

d   Just pull .... here, Miss Gibbs. I'm sorry but you have failed your driving test.
Mel found it difficult to get .... losing her job.
Would you mind if we went .... the proposals one more time?

e   Grimes and Clarke set .... on their expedition to the pole.
After holding .... for several days without food, the escaped prisoner gave himself up.
You don't need to take notes. I'll hand .... summaries of my lecture at the end.

(5 marks)

Total: /50

Unit 10 Test

1 Complete sentences 1–6 with the correct words or phrases (a or b).

1 It's .... surprising that such a .... regarded employee should be promoted.
   a highly   b hardly
2 We have a great local market – you can buy home-made beauty .... and organic .... from local farms.
   a products   b produce
3 We'd be .... if Jerry was here because he'd know exactly what to do, but, unfortunately, he's away .... at the moment.
   a in business   b on business
4 My brother's given me a ticket for the Superbowl, which is a great .... to see my favourite sport, but I'm so busy that there is no .... of me going.
   a opportunity   b possibility
5 The theatre was .... half-full again last night, and, if that continues, we'll .... have to close the show.
   a simply   b barely
6 It was .... cold out on the moors and none of us were .... dressed.
   a adequately   b exceptionally

(12 marks)

2 Read the text about a shopping trip, then answer a–g below.

> Jackie loves going shopping, but doesn't have much money at the moment, so she's just looking. Tracey, on the other hand, was paid yesterday, so she's buying lots of things. She's already bought two T-shirts and three pairs of trainers. Kevin also has three pairs of trainers – but he's stolen them! Darren is at the market trying to buy a second-hand TV. He's offered £50 but the stallholder wants £70. Chelsea, meanwhile, is shopping for the fifth time this week, and she has run up huge bills on her credit cards. Her sister Kelly wants to buy a dress for her birthday party but doesn't want to pay too much – she's already compared dresses and prices in six different shops. And Danny is disappointed. He's been looking for Ken's guitar shop but it closed down two weeks ago.

a Who is on a shopping spree?   ....
b Who has gone out of business?   ....
c Who is shopping around?   ....
d Who is window shopping?   ....
e Who is haggling?   ....
f Who is a shoplifter?   ....
g Who is a shopaholic?   ....

(14 marks)

3 Complete the sentences in a–d, using the word in brackets each time.

a How much do you earn?
I'm not telling you, it's .... ! (business)

b Would you recommend Melissa for the job?
Yes. Of course. I'd .... in recommending her.
(hesitation)

c Do you think we should start the meeting?
Absolutely. Let's .... (business)

d Do you enjoy reading fiction?
Occasionally, but .... I prefer non-fiction.
(whole)

(8 marks)

4 Find and correct one word in each sentence a–h.

a You're doing very well, but, if I may, I'd like to do a few recommendations.
....

b It's important to keep the recipe the shop assistant gives you in case you
want to return the goods.
....

c They were congratulated on working tiredly to complete the project by the
deadline.
....

d There is no alternate – we have to go ahead with the plan.
....

e Frankly, I don't think much of the government's economical policy.
....

f You can't have passed much time doing this – it's a real dog's dinner!
....

g I'm worried that too many people will have access to my personnel details
on the Internet.
....

h Frank likes to haggle off the price with shopkeepers. He's always looking for
a bargain.
....

(16 marks)

Total: /50

Unit 11 Test

1 Match a–e with the sets of words (1–5) that are best associated with them.

a songwriter ....
b painter ....
c author ....
d filmmaker ....
e theatre director ....

1	easel	gallery	canvas
2	premiere	scene	soundtrack
3	lyrics	tunes	hit
4	performance	rehearsal	show
5	plot	page	chapter

(5 marks)

2 Match people a–e with what the thing they are most likely to be looking at (1–5).

a audience ....
b spectator ....
c witness ....
d observer ....
e viewer ....

1 an accident
2 a debate at the United Nations
3 a play
4 a TV programme
5 a tennis match

(5 marks)

3 Complete the gaps in a–e with words from exercises 1 and 2 in the correct form.

a It was the world .... of his new play and a star-studded .... had turned up to watch.
b Millions of .... tuned in to watch *Dangerous Situations*, largely because of its exciting .... which had so many unexpected twists and turns.
c There was a fire at the .... last night in which many paintings were destroyed – a .... said that it was a terrible sight.
d The well-known .... , Tim Noodles, was asked to provide the music for the .... of the film.
e In the opening .... of the film, an explosion at an ice hockey match sends the .... running out of the stadium in panic.

(20 marks)

4 Replace the phrases in italics (1–10) with three-part phrasal verbs made from these verbs and particles.

put	keep	do	make	get	go	stick	run	come
fall	up	on	with	for	out	away	of	at

Most of the time, people in my family .... (1) *have a good relationship with* each other. There are exceptions though. Auntie Mary is constantly (2) .... *criticising* Uncle Frank. I don't know how he .... (3) *bears* her constant nagging. Sometimes I wish he would .... (4) *say or do something in support of* himself. But no, he just smiles good-naturedly whatever she says. Last week Aunty Mary decided to .... (5) *throw out* the new curtains even though she had only just bought them, but Uncle Frank didn't complain. In fact he .... (6) *did something good to apologise for* not buying the right curtains by buying even more expensive ones! Far from .... (7) *becoming short of* patience, Uncle Frank seems to spend most of his time trying to .... (8) *invent* new ways to please my aunt. She is always .... (9) *having arguments with* her daughter Emma, too. She's always telling her off because she isn't .... (10) *learning at the same speed as* the rest of her class at school.

(10 marks)

5 Choose the correct word or phrase (a–c) to complete the responses in 1–5.

1 What was the film like?
Well, it was really exciting. I was on the edge of my seat. In other words, it was ....

    a gripping   b grasping   c growling

2 What was the acting like?
To be honest, awful. The actors showed no emotion, and it was as if they were reading straight from the script. They were very ....

    a hard   b wooden   c heavy

3 Do you get on with your flatmates?
No, not really. We argue a lot but I tend to .... them for a quiet life!

    a give out to   b give in to   c give away to

4 Did you see the street performers?
Yes. Great, weren't they? I watched them for a bit with a group of other ....

    a observers   b onlookers   c witnesses

5 Did you know that Jack is acting in a movie?
Oh, yeah! You see him standing in the background for two minutes. He's not an actor. He's an ....

    a easel   b extra   c artist

(10 marks)

Total: /50

Unit 12 Test

1 Complete sentences a–h with a phrase using the words in brackets.

a Unfortunately there weren't many spectators.
Unfortunately spectators were .... (ground)

b My best friend loves skiing, but nothing would make me do it.
My best friend loves skiing, but I wouldn't do it ....
(world)

c The view from the summit is spectacular.
The view from the summit is .... (world)

d It may be your favourite restaurant, but it's incredibly expensive!
It may be your favourite restaurant, but it .... !
(earth)

e This is a picture of my sister – I absolutely adore her!
This is a picture of my sister – I .... ! (world)

f I needed that holiday. It made me feel much better.
That holiday did me .... (world)

g It was a good idea, but sadly the project was unsuccessful.
The project didn't .... (ground)

h I like Katy, but she always seems to be day-dreaming.
Katy always seems to be .... (world)

(16 marks)

2 Circle the correct word in italics for 1–10 in this article about a pop group.

ENDGAME: the world tour

Winning 'The Y Factor' (1) *generated/provided* a huge amount of interest in this exciting new band, so (2) *promoting/causing* their first world tour shouldn't be too demanding. Band members are (3) *currently/irregularly* rehearsing for the tour.

'It's amazing,' said lead singer Gary. 'Our success has been so exciting – (4) *out of/over* this world! A year ago, hardly anyone came to our concerts and we had a lot of (5) *world/ground* to make up, but now we have fans everywhere. We feel great – on top of the (6) *earth/world*!'

Drummer Andy agrees. 'Last year, we could hardly get a booking, and played together very (7) *progressively/infrequently*. But since our success in 'The Y Factor' we have been playing (8) *increasingly/now and then*. And our success has grown (9) *more and more/hardly ever* with every month. It's been tough at times, but I wouldn't have (10) *missed/lost* it for the world!'

(10 marks)

 photocopiable

3 Choose the correct word or phrase (a, b or c) to complete sentences 1–8.

1 I fill in my tax return every April, in other words I do it ....
   a constantly   b annually   c presently

2 The publishers are trying to .... interest in the new book by organising promotional tours.
   a generate   b imitate   c provide

3 I hate getting wet, so .... would persuade me to go diving.
   a a lot of ground   b nothing on earth   c not in the world

4 I've only seen him twice in the last three years, so I'd have to say that we keep in touch only ....
   a rarely   b annually   c currently

5 Over the last six months, Elsie's condition has .... She's very ill now.
   a promoted   b worsened   c generated

6 Musical styles .... from one country to another, so there's a wide range to enjoy.
   a reduce   b progress   c vary

7 I'm sorry, I haven't understood a word – what .... are you talking about?
   a on the ground   b in the earth   c on earth

8 Over the last decade, the trend has grown for young people to .... demand more freedom in their lives.
   a increasingly   b intermittently   c infrequently

(16 marks)

4 Find and correct one incorrect word in each sentence.

a I like nothing more than spending a weekend fishing of time to time.
   ....

b *Endgame*'s new album is disappointing – it hasn't exactly set the earth on fire.   ....

c Our store caters of people who want fashionable clothes at a reasonable price.   ....

d I don't see much of my housemates as I'm working nights in the moment.
   ....

(8 marks)

Total: /50

Unit Tests Key

Unit 1

1
a 2
b 6
c 1
d 9
e 7
f 5
g 8
h 10
i 3
j 4
(10 marks)

2
1 b
2 c
3 b
4 c
5 b
(5 marks)

3
a vague
b sensible
c thick-skinned
d conscientious
e introvert
(5 marks)

4
1 extrovert
2 thoughtful
3 logical
4 enthusiastic
5 inquisitive
(5 marks)

5
a beginner's
b push
c out
d draw
e stroke
(5 marks)

1 e
2 d
3 a
4 b
5 c
(5 marks)

6
1 on
2 on
3 to
4 to
5 in
(5 marks)

7
a Future Continuous
b Past Continuous
c Past Perfect Simple
d Present Perfect Continuous
e Present Continuous
(10 marks)

Unit 2

1
a 3
b 5
c 4
d 1
e 2
(5 marks)

2
a be bitterly disappointed
b am/'m deeply grateful
c have been absolutely amazed
d doesn't meet with your approval
e break your word
(10 marks)

3
a unforgettable
b revelation
c carving
d amazed
e requirements
(10 marks)

4
1 b
2 f
3 g
4 c
5 k
6 e
7 l
8 m
9 h
10 d
(20 marks)

5
a 3
b 5
c 4
d 2
e 1
(5 marks)

Unit 3

1
1 a
2 a
3 a
4 b
5 a
(10 marks)

2
a as old as the hills
b an old head on young shoulders
c make his mark (in life)
d in the long run
e young at heart
(10 marks)

3
1 with
2 in
3 up
4 make
5 beat
6 make
7 better
8 in
9 down
10 lacking
(10 marks)

4 True: a, b, d, e, h
(10 marks)

5
a Kate
b Carl
c Jake
d Paul
e Mark
(10 marks)

Unit 4

1
a tusk
b horn
c mane
d beak
e paw
f shell
(12 marks)

2
a Edward
b Jane
c Pete
d Jane
e Edward
f Pete
g Jane, Edward
(16 marks)

3
a out
b to
c for
d with
e off
f at
g at
(14 marks)

4
1 c
2 c
3 b
4 a
(8 marks)

Unit 5

1
a 1
b 2
c 5
d 8
e 4
f 3
g 7
h 9
i 6
j 10
(10 marks)

2
a cheek
b ribs
c wrist
d shin
e waist
(10 marks)

3
a 2
b 4
c 3
d 5
e 1
(5 marks)

4
a dislocated shoulder
b searing pain
c toothache
d high temperature
e fractured skull
(5 marks)

5
a survival
b intolerable
c threatening
d technological
e avoidable
f mechanic
g (un)acceptable
h explanation
i predictions
j memorable
(20 marks)

Unit 6

1
a limped
b plodded
c crept
d hobbled/limped
e staggered
(5 marks)

2
a 4
b 7
c 9
d 5
e 1
f 8
g 10
h 2
i 3
j 6
(5 marks)

3
a ~~get~~ come
b ~~less~~ little
c ~~false~~ left
d ~~of~~ to
e ~~off~~ back
f ~~mood~~ sense
g ~~with~~ about
h ~~foot~~ hand
(16 marks)

4
a ring true
b more than likely
c in the right
d sooner or later
e under false pretences
f more or less
g before long
h right away
(16 marks)

5
1 a
2 a
3 a
4 b
(8 marks)

Unit 7

1
a unsuitable, responsible for
b illegal, resulted in
c set off, international
d indecisive, putting off
e misinformed, effect on
f dishonest, lead to
g turn the oven off, overcooked
h source of, irrelevant.
i illogical, put off
j independent, give in/up
(20 marks)

2
a taken in
b set off
c put off
d put (me) off
e give in
f turn off
(6 marks)

3
a beneficial
b accuracy
c evidence
d immoral
e inspirational/inspiring
f dramatic
g awareness
(14 marks)

4 One of the most (1)**significant** hurricanes of recent times was 'Katrina' which was responsible for battering the coast of Louisiana in the USA in September 2005, causing untold (2)**devastation**. Local authorities were not prepared as they had

(3)**underestimated** the strength of the hurricane. The force of the storm resulted in a number of breaches in the protection system of New Orleans, which in turn led to flooding so (4)**catastrophic** and extensive that it will take years for the city to recover. Emergency services worked tirelessly during the storm, refusing to give in, but they were (5)**incapable** of stopping the flooding.
(10 marks)

Unit 8

1   a   4
   b   1
   c   5
   d   2
   e   8
   f   3
   g   6
   h   7
(16 marks)

2   a   out of
   b   in
   c   in
   d   In
   e   at
   f   out of
   g   to
   h   on
(16 marks)

3   1   c
   2   g
   3   e
   4   h
   5   f
   6   a
   7   b
   8   d
(8 marks)

4   a   principles
   b   momentous
   c   term
   d   means
   e   spur
   f   controversial
   g   weigh
   h   loose
   i   Antisocial
   j   overpopulated
(10 marks)

Unit 9

1   a   3
   b   10
   c   6
   d   1
   e   4
   f   2
   g   5
   h   8
   i   7
   j   9
(10 marks)

2   a   6
   b   4
   c   7
   d   3
   e   1
   f   5
   g   2
(14 marks)

3   1   a
   2   b
   3   a
   4   a
   5   b
(5 marks)

4   1   d
   2   f
   3   g
   4   a
   5   h
   6   c
   7   b
   8   e
(16 marks)

5   a   out
   b   for
   c   of
   d   over
   e   out
(5 marks)

Unit 10

1   1   b, a
   2   a, b
   3   a, b
   4   a, b
   5   b, a
   6   b, a
(12 marks)

2   a   Tracy
   b   Ken
   c   Kelly
   d   Jackie
   e   Darren
   f   Kevin
   g   Chelsea
(14 marks)

3   a   none of your business
   b   have no hesitation
   c   get down to business
   d   on the whole
(8 marks)

4   a   You're doing very well, but, if I may, I'd like to **make** a few recommendations.
   b   It's important to keep the **receipt** the shop assistant gives you in case you want to return the goods.
   c   They were congratulated on working **tirelessly** to complete the project by the deadline.
   d   There is no **alternative** – we have to go ahead with the plan.
   e   Frankly, I don't think much of the government's **economic** policy.
   f   You can't have **spent** much time doing this – it's a real dog's dinner!
   g   I'm worried that other people will have access to my **personal** details if I shop on the Internet.

h   Frank likes to haggle over the price with shopkeepers. He's always looking for a bargain.

(16 marks)

Unit 11

1 a   3
    b   1
    c   5
    d   2
    e   4
(5 marks)

2 a   3
    b   5
    c   1
    d   2
    e   4
(5 marks)

3 a   premiere, audience
    b   viewers, plot
    c   gallery, witness
    d   songwriter, soundtrack
    e   scene, spectators
(20 marks)

4 1   get on with
    2   going on at
    3   puts up with
    4   stick up for
    5   do away with
    6   made up for
    7   running out of
    8   come up with
    9   falling out with
    10 keeping up with
(10 marks)

5 1   a
    2   b
    3   b
    4   b
    5   c
(10 marks)

Unit 12

1 a   thin on the ground
    b   for the world
    c   out of this world
    d   costs the earth
    e   think the world of her
    f   did me the world of good
    g   get off the ground
    h   in a world of her own
(16 marks)

2 1   generated
    2   promoting
    3   currently
    4   out of
    5   ground
    6   world
    7   infrequently
    8   increasingly
    9   more and more
    10 missed
(10 marks)

3 1   b
    2   a
    3   b
    4   a
    5   b
    6   c
    7   c
    8   a
(16 marks)

4 a   I like nothing more than spending a weekend fishing **from** time to time.
    b   *Endgame*'s new album is disappointing – it hasn't exactly set the **world** on fire.
    c   Our store caters **for** people who want fashionable clothes at a reasonable price.
    d   I don't see much of my housemates as I'm working nights **at** the moment.
(8 marks)

Progress Test 1
Units 1–3

1 Read the text about a Hollywood legend and choose the correct word in 1–8.

RUDOLPH VALENTINO

After Rudolph Valentino's (1) *death/dead*, more than 100,000 people lined the streets of New York for his funeral. It was 1926, and the young star died from (2) *complicated/complications* following a double operation for appendicitis, and stomach ulcers. Valentino had been the most popular (3) *romance/romantic* leading man of the silent era of Hollywood movies, and almost (4) *each/every* young woman in America was heartbroken when he died. Valentino arrived in the U.S. from Italy in 1913. After (5) *danceing/dancing* professionally in New York, he set off for California, where he soon received bit parts in movies and became typecast as the (6) *villainous/villian* foreign seducer. In 1921, he got his big breakthrough in the film *The Four Horsemen of the Apocalypse* produced by Rex Ingrams. This was considered a (7) *main/major* achievement and one of the first anti-war films. Tragically, within five years the star's career and life were over, but Valentino is still (8) *remembered/memorised* as one of Hollywood's most enduring legends.

(16 marks)

2 Read the text below and circle the best option (A, B, C, or D) to complete gaps 1–12.

School sports day

When I was at school, sports day was the highlight of the year. Let me .... (1) the scene. First of all, on sports day, it was always bound .... (2) rain. Sunny weather? No such luck. Despite the previous two months of soaring temperatures, as likely .... (3) not, on the morning of the games, the temperature would plummet. So, imagine a hundred .... (4) small children, dressed in tight shorts and thin vests, shivering in the cold, unaware of the heartbreak that .... (5) in store for them. Swept .... (6) by the excitement and desperate to win, tempers soon get .... (7). One girl finds herself disqualified from the egg and spoon race despite giving it everything she's got, and another boy, ... (8) jealous of the winner of the sack race, makes the mistake of being rude to him .... (9) earshot of the teachers. Scores of tiny children, ... (10) disappointed at tasting defeat for the first time, break down and cry. Twenty years on, I'm certainly not .... (11) any younger, but I do have some really lasting .... (12) of those days at school!

1	A	put	B	set	C	make	D	do
2	A	for	B	of	C	by	D	to
3	A	to	B	if	C	as	D	than
4	A	enthusiast	B	enthusiastic	C	enthuse	D	enthusiasm
5	A	sits	B	stands	C	lies	D	hides
6	A	over	B	up	C	down	D	off
7	A	fractured	B	turned	C	frayed	D	torn
8	A	fiercely	B	warmly	C	keenly	D	strongly
9	A	between	B	within	C	among	D	across
10	A	absolutely	B	strongly	C	warmly	D	bitterly
11	A	getting	B	putting	C	going	D	coming
12	A	remembrances	B	mementoes	C	souvenirs	D	memories

(12 marks)

3 For a–j, rewrite the part of the sentence in italics with a phrase using the words in brackets.

a I am writing to you *as the representative of* the Manager. (behalf)

....

b My grandfather *started* the company in 1956. (set)

....

c I can't tell you how *much I appreciate* your help. (grateful)

....

d Modern fashions are not *something that I like*. (taste)

....

e It's *very likely* that the government will change the law. (cards)

....

f In the ten minutes he was on the pitch, the substitute certainly *had an impact*. (mark)

....

g *As well as* her day job in an office, Sheila also works in the evenings. (addition)

....

h Try to be optimistic. I'm sure better times *will soon be on their way*. (corner)

....

i The police arrived to *put a stop to* the demonstration. (break)

....

j We all hope that, *eventually*, this new policy will be successful. (run)

....

(10 marks)

4 Complete sentences a–l with one word formed from the word in capitals.

a You can trust Gary completely. He's the most .... person I know. RELY

b It's important to be .... when giving someone bad news. TACT

c Jo's invaluable .... made the scheme a success. CONTRIBUTE

d Jack is a very .... little boy, constantly asking questions. INQUIRE

e I have no .... in recommending Paula for the position. HESITATE

f Nursing has a reputation as one of the most .... of professions. CARE

g There was no hint of .... when I showed him the photograph. RECOGNISE

h It was a(n) .... day, and one we'll both treasure forever. FORGET

i You wouldn't have failed the exam if you hadn't approached it so .... CARE

j Please let us know of any special medical .... at the time of booking. REQUIRE

k What do you think is the best .... of someone's success? INDICATE

l This position really needs a .... person. DECIDE

(12 marks)

Total: /50

Progress Test 2
Units 4–6

1 For each of a–j, circle the correct word (A, B, C or D) to complete the sentence.

a We were driving home when all .... a sudden we got a puncture.
  A on   B at   C of   D with

b Tom was the only male in the aerobics class – he felt like a real .... out of water.
  A whale   B dolphin   C shark   D fish

c Charlotte was really unwell for a few days, but, fortunately she's on the .... now.
  A move   B fix   C mend   D repair

d Frankly, Jenny's explanation doesn't .... true. I don't believe her for a moment.
  A ring   B call   C come   D look

e Students often feel apprehensive .... leaving home and going to university.
  A besides   B about   C around   D towards

f If you keep taking risks like that, you'll end up hurting yourself before ....
  A long   B soon   C far   D later

g I'll come and help, but I'm not doing all the .... work while you mess around!
  A horse   B dog   C donkey   D elephant

h The weather forecasters say it's more than .... we'll have gales at the weekend.
  A certain   B rights   C likely   D true

i Sadly, the .... of many species in the wild is already in doubt.
  A survive   B survival   C surviving   D survivor

j Why not take the day off work if you're feeling .... the weather?
  A beyond   B over   C above   D under

(10 marks)

2 Read the text below and circle the best option (A, B, C, or D) to complete gaps 1–12.

THE BLACK SEA

Arriving in the Black Sea port of Batumi was a dream .... (1) true for me. For years I had longed to wander slowly along the promenade .... (2) out over this landlocked sea, so as I headed to the coast, with .... (3) in my stomach, I felt both excited and strangely nervous. Would the Black Sea actually be black? Well, I'll .... (4) the cat out of the bag – it isn't! And, according .... (5) my guidebook, the Black Sea is more like a lake than a sea. It has no tides, and, thanks to modern technology, we now know that below a certain depth it is too poisonous to sustain life. But its calm surface gives a false .... (6); on stormy days, the churning waters can have a .... (7) effect on shipping.

My travelling companion and I had bought cheap tickets on the overnight train from Tbilisi, the capital of Georgia. This had proved to be a .... (8) economy as we hardly got any sleep, and by the time we arrived in Batumi, we were so tired and hungry that we virtually .... (9) off the train. We had a few .... (10) to eat from the previous night's meal but nothing appetising. That first evening though, we had a very agreeable time, drinking Georgian wine, excited .... (11) the thought of being by the sea where once, ... (12) the sudden storms, Ancient Greeks traded and Byzantine ships patrolled the shores.

1	A	gone	B	come	C	taken	D	done
2	A	gazing	B	glancing	C	peeping	D	glimpsing
3	A	birds	B	butterflies	C	moths	D	bees
4	A	allow	B	lose	C	leave	D	let
5	A	for	B	at	C	to	D	with
6	A	idea	B	pretence	C	impression	D	sense
7	A	beneficial	B	threatening	C	crucial	D	devastating
8	A	cheap	B	false	C	true	D	fake
9	A	strolled	B	skipped	C	marched	D	staggered
10	A	leftovers	B	deposits	C	relics	D	remains
11	A	for	B	with	C	at	D	in
12	A	in spite	B	although	C	despite	D	nevertheless

(12 marks)

3 For a–h complete the second sentence so that it has a similar meaning to the first sentence, using the word in brackets in the correct form. Use between two and five words, including the word given.

a The accident happened when two cars crashed into each other.   (collide)

   The accident happened when two cars .... another.

b Smethurst knew that eventually the police would catch him.   (soon)

   Smethurst knew that .... the police would catch him.

c Tracy always seems to be daydreaming.   (world)

   Tracy always seems to be .... her own.

d Just wait a moment. I'll return immediately.   (right)

   Just wait a moment. I'll ....

e We're getting a present for Tim but it's a surprise so don't tell him! (cat)

   We're getting a present for Tim but it's a surprise so don't let the .... !

f Both Tom and Andy went to the film premiere.   (well)

   Tom, ... , went to to the film premiere.

g In recent years the economy has been gradually improving.   (little)

   In recent years the economy has been improving ....

h My sister was unwell last week, but she's getting better now. (mend)

   My sister was unwell last week, but she's .... now.

(16 marks)

4 For a–l, write the word being defined.

a The part of a fish which controls the direction it moves in.   ....

b To walk slowly with weak, unsteady steps, e.g. when you are sick.   ....

c The hard outer casing of a tortoise, crab, etc.   ....

d How you might walk if you have injured your leg or foot.   ....

e The equivalent of a foot on a horse, cow, etc.   ....

f To move on your hands and knees across the floor.   ....

g The bone at the front of the leg below the knee.   ....

h To put a part of the body out of its joint.   ....

i Another word for a 'feeler' on an insect.   ....

j The tough skin of an animal such as an elephant.   ....

k To take a quick look at something you shouldn't really see.   ....

l The joint that gives flexibility to the hand.   ....

(12 marks)

Total:	/50

Progress Test 3
Units 7–9

1 Read the text below, then complete gaps 1–16 with the correct form of the word in brackets.

Rising crime?

In recent months, there has been a growing .... (1 perceive) among the general public that crime in this country is on the increase. .... (2 drama) newspaper headlines imply that somebody is being murdered around every corner, but the .... (3 evident) simply doesn't add up. The truth is that crimes such as .... (4 burgle) have declined considerably in the last year, suggesting that contrary to popular opinion, the nation is not as .... (5 moral) as some appear to believe, and not everybody is living next door to a violent .... (6 mug). There has been some fairly .... (7 decide) action by the police.

In a .... (8 controversy) move last year, they intitiated a policy of getting tough on persistent young .... (9 offence), and they have had a .... (10 signify) amount of success in this area. Moreover, the .... (11 appear) of more policemen on the streets has almost certainly kept crime levels low. Nobody wants to .... (12 estimate) the impact of crime on its victims, but the simple truth is that crime is not .... (13 extend) in this country, by any means, and much of the fear of crime is .... (14 logic). If the public's .... (15 aware) of this fact were to increase, it would undoubtedly be extremely .... (16 benefit) for everybody.

(16 marks)

2 Find and correct one mistake in each of sentences a–k.

a These days, I'm incapable for climbing the stairs, never mind a mountain! ....

b We are on a loose end – I wonder whether we could come and see you. ....

c The commission found that nobody was responsible of the accident. ....

d Mark is impulsive – he's always taking decisions at the spur of the moment. ....

e One of the principle arguments for the scheme is that it would save money. ....

f In the very end of the book, the two lovers meet up one last time. ....

g Don't be taken up by his charming manner – he's very untrustworthy. ....

h The accused was charged of assault and causing criminal damage. ....

i The fall of the Berlin Wall was one of the momentary events of the 20th century. ....

j Have you managed to find a volunteer to set over the fireworks? ....

k My neighbour was taken to custody by the police! ....

(11 marks)

3 For each of a–k circle the correct word (A, B or C) to complete the sentence.

a Nobody expected Sally to resign. It came out of the ....
   A sky   B blue   C dream

b Frank received very little compensation .... the injuries he received in the accident.
   A of   B for   C from

c The construction of the stadium has already taken more than a decade, and there appears to be no end in ....
   A sight   B touch   C hand

d Although the new restaurant has had sensational reviews, we've been .... by its extremely high prices.
   A set off   B put off   C given off

e I wonder what the source .... all these startling revelations is.
   A from   B of   C for

f It won't help in the long run but it provides a useful short- .... solution.
   A haul   B term   C form

g Going to war was a(n) .... decision as so few people in the country were in favour of it.
   A unsocial   B controversial   C trivial

h The media are accusing the government of .... the public in what they say is a deliberate cover-up.
   A underestimating   B unfastening   C misinforming

i The government are trying to stamp down on .... behaviour such as vandalism.
   A antisocial   B momentous   C dishonest

j Daly was arrested for accepting a .... to deliberately lose the boxing match.
   A bribe   B blackmail   C forgery

k Someone ran .... in front of my car and I nearly had an accident.
   A off   B by   C out

(11 marks)

4 Read the text below and circle the best option (A, B, C, or D) to complete gaps 1–12.

Traffic calming

The aim of this town council meeting is to discuss whether there is scope .... (1) the introduction of traffic calming measures in this area. Joy-riding is to blame .... (2) a significant reduction in the quality of life on the housing estates, and has directly led .... (3) the deaths of two young people. We must stop this menace before it gets out of control. The best interests of our community are .... (4) stake.

My personal view of the choices before us is that we should not give .... (5) to lawlessness on our streets, nor should we be put .... (6) by the costs of introducing stringent traffic calming measures. .... (7) the long run, I believe that the result .... (8) taking action now will mean safer streets for everyone. And, of course, if we take no action, we will more than likely end up .... (9) with more deaths.

To .... (10) up, spending on traffic calming is vitally needed. By all means, weigh .... (11) the pros and cons. Having done so, however, I'm sure you will agree that, ... (12) balance, a little money spent today will prove to be a good investment.

1	A for	B of		C that		D to
2	A in	B on		C by		D for
3	A to	B into		C on		D by
4	A on	B at		C in		D for
5	A in	B over		C up		D away
6	A up	B off		C away		D down
7	A At	B On		C In		D For
8	A of	B for		C that		D with
9	A with	B at		C in		D by
10	A add	B sum		C total		D give
11	A out	B up		C over		D in
12	A in	B with		C by		D on

(12 marks)

Total: /50

Progress Test 4
Units 10–12

1 Find the extra incorrect word or missing word in 1–15. Cross out the incorrect word or write in the missing word.

   1 Whilst away on a business I recently came across a wonderful book about the origins of words.

   2 I haggled the price for a while before finally buying it.

   3 Fortunately, it didn't cost the whole earth.

   4 Being a linguist, I like to keep with ideas about where expressions come from.

   5 So I simply barely had to have this book.

   6 Researchers think up new theories about word origins, or 'etymology', all at the time.

   7 Sometimes I think the ideas that they come up to with are rather fanciful.

   8 An example that I find fascinating is the often everyday word 'OK'.

   9 It is hardly surprising that theories about it are not thin about on the ground.

   10 Almost hardly anyone agrees on its derivation.

   11 It could be from the Greek *ola kala*, or the Democratic OK Club, set up with in 1840 to promote their presidential candidate from a place called 'Old Kinderhook'.

   12 On whole, these theories are all equally plausible.

   13 We'll probably never run out new suggestions.

   14 Neither will we ever be sure where on the earth this curious word comes from.

   15 But I'm sure the OK Club candidate would have felt on top of all the world, and not just OK, to be associated with it!

   (15 marks)

2 For a–f complete the second sentence so that it has a similar meaning to the first sentence, using the word in brackets in the correct form. Use between two and five words, including the word given.

   a I'd like to invite you to dinner to say sorry for forgetting your birthday. (make)

      I'd like to .... your birthday by inviting you to dinner.

   b Joe's café has closed because it wasn't making any money. (business)

      Joe's café ....

   c Jill and I go for a stroll in the countryside occasionally. (time)

      Jill and I go for a stroll in the countryside ....

d Guests are welcome to suggest any improvements at Reception. (recommendations)

Guests are welcome to ……………………………………………… improvements at Reception.

e I would be very happy to employ your company in future. (hesitation)

I would have ……………………………………………… your company in future.

f It looks like it might be sunny later. (possibility)

There ……………………………………………… sunshine later.

(12 marks)

3 For each of 1–11, circle the option (A, B or C) which best describes the situation.

1 Mandy and her friends spent all afternoon looking at clothes but didn't buy anything.
A shoplifting   B window shopping   C shopping around

2 At last the local council have got rid of those dreadful old park benches.
A They've done away   B They've run out of them.   C They've put up
   with them.   with them.

3 Only 52% of people voted for the new president.
A That's highly half.   B That's simply half.   C That's barely half.

4 We watched an incredibly thrilling film last night.
A It was awkward.   B It was gripping.   C It was wooden.

5 Two passers-by happened to be at the scene when the tragedy occurred.
A They were witnesses.   B They were viewers.   C They were onlookers.

6 The actors are on stage, going over their lines one last time.
A It's the first night.   B It's a rehearsal.   C It's the premiere.

7 Our accountants start working the minute they reach the office each day.
A They get down to   B They go out of business.   C They go on business.
   business.

8 We apologise but the website you are trying to view is presently unavailable.
A It's infrequently available.   B It's currently unavailable.   C It's intermittently available.

9 Does your car cost much to keep on the road?
A Is it economic?   B Is it eco-friendly?   C Is it economical?

10 My grandfather used to write the words for songs, but not the music.
A He wrote tunes.   B He wrote lyrics.   C He wrote soundtracks.

11 I was walking down the street when a man ran by and took my purse!
A There was a mugging.   B There was a burglary.   C There was a forgery.

(11 marks)

4 Read the text below and circle the best option (A, B, C, or D) to complete gaps 1–12.

My father, a .... (1) regarded member of the legal profession, was not generally an early riser, but he made an exception every January 2nd for what was a(n) .... (2) event in our family – queueing for the January sales. At any other time of the year, my father hardly .... (3) shopped, and if he did, he would shop around before making any purchases, but on this one day a year he would make up .... (4) his normal reticence by simply grabbing bargains off the shelves at random.

My mother was always going .... (5) at him for buying useless things .... (6) because they were half the original asking price. For example, we never quite worked out why on .... (7) he once decided to buy an entire range of gardening .... (8) despite the fact we lived in an apartment with no garden. On another occasion he drew a crowd of curious .... (9) as he struggled to get on a bus carrying a stuffed bear. The passengers must have been utterly astonished to see such a sight boarding the vehicle.

While .... (10) on earth would tempt me to hang around in the cold waiting for the shops to open, I'm inclined to .... (11) up for my father and his odd behaviour. I think it was a form of light relief for him from his stressful job, and did him the world of .... (12). Not only that, but, from to time to time, he did actually buy something really useful!

1	A hardly	B fairly	C highly	D tirelessly
2	A current	B annual	C present	D constant
3	A ever	B never	C often	D always
4	A from	B with	C in	D for
5	A out	B up	C on	D off
6	A plainly	B simply	C utterly	D exceptionally
7	A world	B earth	C ground	D the world
8	A productions	B produce	C products	D producers
9	A onlookers	B viewers	C audience	D witnesses
10	A anything	B something	C nothing	D not
11	A put	B stick	C set	D weigh
12	A fun	B happiness	C good	D joy

(12 marks)

Total:	/50

Answer key

Progress Test 1

1
1 death
2 complications
3 romantic
4 every
5 dancing
6 villainous
7 major
8 remembered

(16 marks)

2
1 B
2 D
3 C
4 B
5 C
6 B
7 C
8 A
9 B
10 D
11 A
12 D

(12 marks)

3
a on behalf of
b set up
c grateful I am for
d to my taste
e on the cards
f made his mark
g In addition to
h are just (a)round the corner
i break up
j in the long run

(10 marks)

4
a reliable
b tactful
c contribution
d inquisitive
e hesitation
f caring
g recognition
h unforgettable
i carelessly
j requirements
k indicator
l decisive

(12 marks)

Progress Test 2

1
a C
b D
c C
d A
e B
f A
g C
h C
i B
j D

(10 marks)

2
1 B
2 A
3 B
4 D
5 C
6 C
7 D
8 B
9 D
10 A
11 C
12 C

(12 marks)

3
a collided with one
b sooner or later
c in a world of
d be right back
e cat out of the bag
f as well as Andy
g little by little
h on the mend

(16 marks)

4
a fin
b stagger
c shell
d limp
e hoof
f crawl
g shin
h dislocate
i antenna
j hide
k peep
l wrist

(12 marks)

Progress Test 3

1
1 perception
2 dramatic
3 evidence
4 burglary/burglaries
5 immoral
6 mugger
7 decisive
8 controversial
9 offenders
10 significant
11 appearance
12 underestimate
13 extensive
14 illogical
15 awareness
16 beneficial

(16 marks)

2
a incapable **of**
b **at a loose end**
c responsible **for**
d **on the spur of the moment**
e **principal**
f **At the very end**
g taken **in** by
h charged **with**
i **momentous** events
j set **off**
k taken **into**

(11 marks)

3
a B
b B
c A
d B
e B
f B
g B
h C
i A
j A
k C

(11 marks)

4
1 A
2 D
3 A
4 B
5 A
6 B
7 C
8 A
9 A
10 B
11 B
12 D

(12 marks)

Progress Test 4

1
1 ~~a~~ business
2 haggled <u>over</u>
3 ~~whole~~ earth
4 keep <u>up</u>
5 simply ~~barely~~
6 ~~at~~ the time
7 come up ~~to~~
8 ~~often~~ everyday
9 thin ~~about~~
10 ~~Almost~~ hardly
11 set up ~~with~~
12 On <u>the</u> whole
13 run out <u>of</u>
14 on ~~the~~ earth
15 ~~all~~ the world

(15 marks)

2
a make up for forgetting
b has gone out of business
c from time to time
d make any recommendations for
e no hesitation in employing
f is a/the possiblity of

(12 marks)

3
1 B
2 A
3 C
4 B
5 A
6 B
7 A
8 B
9 C
10 B
11 A

(11 marks)

4
1 C
2 B
3 A
4 D
5 C
6 B
7 B
8 C
9 A
10 C
11 B
12 C

(12 marks)

UNIVERSITY *of* **CAMBRIDGE**
ESOL Examinations

Candidate Name
If not already printed, write name
in CAPITALS and complete the
Candidate No. grid (in pencil).

Candidate Signature

SAMPLE

Examination Title

Centre

Supervisor:

If the candidate is ABSENT or has WITHDRAWN shade here

Centre No.

Candidate No.

Examination Details

0	0	0	0
1	1	1	1
2	2	2	2
3	3	3	3
4	4	4	4
5	5	5	5
6	6	6	6
7	7	7	7
8	8	8	8
9	9	9	9

Candidate Answer Sheet

Instructions

Use a PENCIL (B or HB).

Mark ONE letter for each question.

For example, if you think B is the right answer to the question, mark your answer sheet like this:

Rub out any answer you wish to change using an eraser.

1	A B C D E F G H
2	A B C D E F G H
3	A B C D E F G H
4	A B C D E F G H
5	A B C D E F G H
6	A B C D E F G H
7	A B C D E F G H
8	A B C D E F G H
9	A B C D E F G H
10	A B C D E F G H
11	A B C D E F G H
12	A B C D E F G H
13	A B C D E F G H
14	A B C D E F G H
15	A B C D E F G H
16	A B C D E F G H
17	A B C D E F G H
18	A B C D E F G H
19	A B C D E F G H
20	A B C D E F G H

21	A B C D E F G H
22	A B C D E F G H
23	A B C D E F G H
24	A B C D E F G H
25	A B C D E F G H
26	A B C D E F G H
27	A B C D E F G H
28	A B C D E F G H
29	A B C D E F G H
30	A B C D E F G H
31	A B C D E F G H
32	A B C D E F G H
33	A B C D E F G H
34	A B C D E F G H
35	A B C D E F G H
36	A B C D E F G H
37	A B C D E F G H
38	A B C D E F G H
39	A B C D E F G H
40	A B C D E F G H

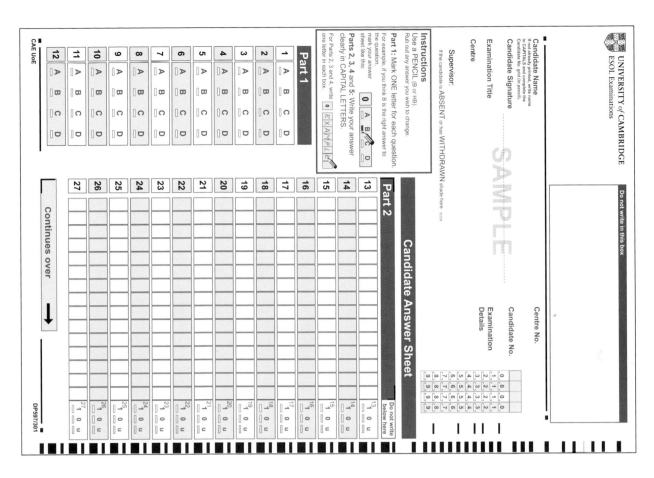

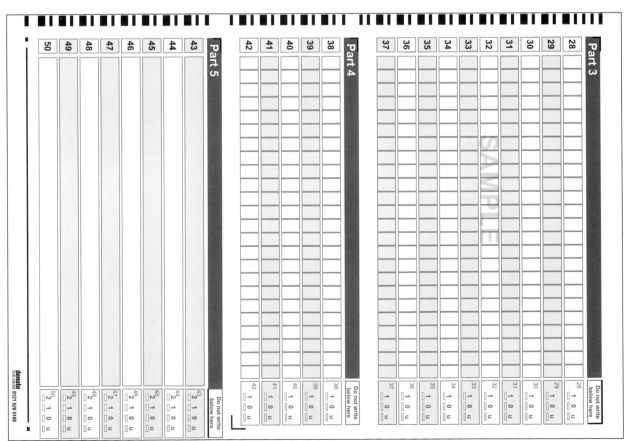

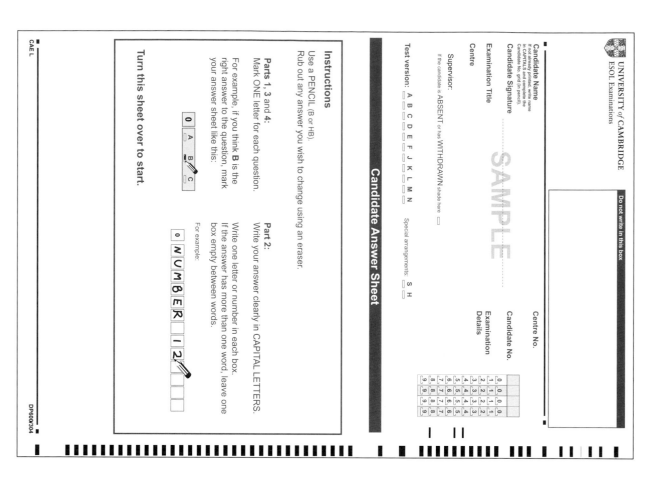

UNIVERSITY of CAMBRIDGE
ESOL Examinations

Do not write in this box

Candidate Name
If not already printed, write name
in CAPITALS and complete the
Candidate No. grid (in pencil).

Candidate Signature

Examination Title

Centre

SAMPLE

Candidate Answer Sheet

Centre No.

Candidate No.

Examination
Details

Supervisor:
If the candidate is ABSENT or has WITHDRAWN shade here

Test version: A B C D E F J K L M N   Special arrangements: S H

Instructions

Use a PENCIL (B or HB).
Rub out any answer you wish to change using an eraser.

Parts 1, 3 and 4:
Mark ONE letter for each question.

For example, if you think **B** is the
right answer to the question, mark
your answer sheet like this:

0   A   B   C

Part 2:
Write your answer clearly in CAPITAL LETTERS.

Write one letter or number in each box.
If the answer has more than one word, leave one
box empty between words.

For example:

0   N U M B E R   1 2

Turn this sheet over to start.

CAE L

DP600/304

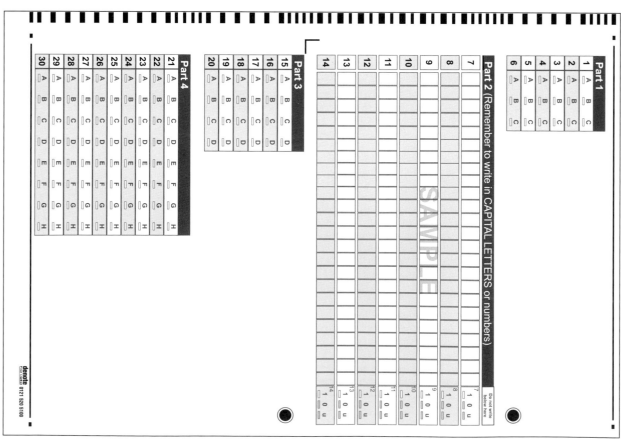

Part 1

1 A B C
2 A B C
3 A B C
4 A B C
5 A B C
6 A B C

Part 2 (Remember to write in CAPITAL LETTERS or numbers)

Do not write
below here

7
8
9
10
11
12
13
14

SAMPLE

Part 3

15 A B C D
16 A B C D
17 A B C D
18 A B C D
19 A B C D
20 A B C D

Part 4

21 A B C D E F G H
22 A B C D E F G H
23 A B C D E F G H
24 A B C D E F G H
25 A B C D E F G H
26 A B C D E F G H
27 A B C D E F G H
28 A B C D E F G H
29 A B C D E F G H
30 A B C D E F G H

denote
Print & Internet
0121 520 5100

oxfordenglishtesting.com

What is oxfordenglishtesting.com?

- It's a website that gives students of English access to interactive practice tests.
- It's where students who have bought OUP Workbook Resource Packs can access online practice tests included in the Pack, and buy more if they wish.

The website will become a gateway for all sorts of English tests available to both students and institutions.

You can register on oxfordenglishtesting.com and try a free sample test to see how it works. A demo is also available from your local OUP office.

What is on the Student's Workbook MultiROM?

The MultiROM has two parts.
- Students can listen to the audio material that accompanies the Workbook by playing the MultiROM in an audio CD player, or in a media player on their computer.
- Students can also access one or two practice tests online with the MultiROM.

More about the tests

The online practice tests reflect what happens in the real exam, in the same way as printed practice tests from Oxford University Press. They include every paper and question that a student will find in the real exam.

With the exception of the Speaking Test, students do not print the tests in order to do them. They take them online and most questions are marked automatically online. In addition, there are help features that students can use. These include dictionary look-up, exam tips, the ability to mark and change individual answers, and get feedback on answers. See test features on the page opposite for more details.

Students have access to each test for three months before they must submit it for final marking. They can choose to do parts of the test, or the whole test at any time during that period. Students can monitor their progress via the **Test Overview** which records questions not attempted, attempted but not marked, questions that cannot be marked online, and right and wrong answers. Students can also print the **Test Overview** and **Results** page.

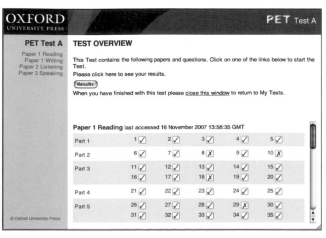

Writing and Speaking papers

The website cannot automatically mark the Writing essay questions and Speaking papers online. The default result will exclude these papers. The result the students see includes totals for each of the parts and a percentage. It also gives an indication as to whether the score is equivalent to a pass or not. Obviously this is a practice test not the real exam and the result is only an indication of what students might achieve in a real exam.

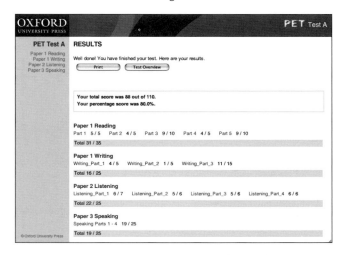

There are *sample answers* for Writing questions which give students an idea of what is expected of them. If you want students to enter a score for essay questions, they can print their essay, or email it to you so that you can mark it. They can then enter their marks into the **Results** page on the website. Their final score will then be adjusted to take the marks into account.

Students get sample Speaking papers and *Useful language* to help them practise offline. The Speaking paper can be printed from the **My tests** page. If you want you can conduct the Speaking Test with students and they can enter their marks into the **Results** page on the website. Their final score will then be adjusted to take the marks into account.

Tests for purchase by teachers and institutions

From September 2008, teachers and institutions will be able to buy and administer practice tests for their students. The tests will be different to those available to students via Workbook Resource Packs or purchased by students online. Teachers will be able to set the tests in practice or test mode, and will be able to record students' results. There will also be a placement test that can be used to determine students' level of English.

For more information go www.oup.com/elt.

There is also a list of Frequently Asked Questions (FAQs) on the website. Go to www.oxfordenglishtesting.com, click on any link to register and then go to the **Support** tab.

What are the features of the test?

Exam tips	There is a tip on how to answer every question.
Dictionary look-up	Students can look up the meaning of any word in the practice test. They just double click it and a definition will pop up. They will need to have pop-up windows enabled.
Instant marking and feedback	When a student has answered a question, they can mark it straight away to see whether they got it right. If the answer was wrong, they can get feedback to find out why it was wrong.
Change your answer or try again	Students can then go back and have another go as many times as they like. Understanding why they answered a question incorrectly helps them think more clearly about a similar question next time.
Save and come back later	Students don't have to complete a Paper in one go. When they log out it saves what they've done. They can come back to it at any time. Students have 90 days before they have to submit the practice test for final marking. The **My tests** page tells students how many days they have left to access the test.
Mark individual answers, a part, a paper or the whole test	However much students have done of the practice test, they can mark it and see how well they're doing.
Audio scripts	These are available for all parts of the Listening test. Reading the audio script will help students understand any areas they didn't understand when they were listening to them.
Sample answers for essay questions in the Writing paper	Students can see *sample answers* after they've written their own. They've been written by real students, and will give them a good idea of what's expected. The essay they write will not be marked automatically. If you would like to mark your student's essay, tell them and they can either print it off to give to you, or email it to you. When you've marked it, they can enter the mark on their **Results** page. It does not matter if they do not enter a mark for the essay. The final marks will be adjusted to take that into account.
Useful phrases for the Speaking paper	Students get sample Speaking papers and *Useful language* to help them practise offline. If you want to assess your students they can print the Speaking paper from the **My tests** page, and ask you to do the Speaking paper with them. As with the Writing paper, you can give them a mark and they can enter the mark on the **Results** page. However, if you don't, their final marks will be adjusted to take that into account.
Results page	Remember this is a practice test not the real exam. Students will see their score by paper and part and as a percentage. This will only be an indication as to whether their score is equivalent to a pass or not.
Try a sample test first	You can try out a short version of a practice test yourself. Go to oxfordenglishtesting.com and click on **Try**. You can also ask your local OUP office for a demo.
Buy more practice tests	To get even more practice, students can buy more tests on oxfordenglishtesting.com